The Fine Art
of Chinese Cooking

The Fine

Art of

~~~~~~

EDITED BY JUNE TAYLOR

JACKET DESIGN AND DECORATIONS

BY JEANYEE WONG

Chinese Cooking

by **DR. LEE SU JAN**
and **MAY LEE**

GRAMERCY PUBLISHING COMPANY • NEW YORK

Preface

I suppose I first fell in love with the Chinese idea of food when I heard the reason for the mid-morning snack: to relieve the monotony of not eating! A people who had developed such an attitude toward food seemed to me to be worth further investigation.

As a people, the Chinese have made time to enjoy the good things of life—no drug store counter lunches for them! Urbane and charming, they love good food. In the happy company of Chinese friends, I have run the gamut from a single cup of tea to a New Year's feast lasting until well after dawn. Now, through the special gifts of the Dr. and Mrs. Lee Su Jan, we are able to learn the simple methods and surprisingly few ingredients necessary to work these miracles of food. Invariably Chinese cooking is delightful, both in flavor and in texture, and has a wonderful aroma. Last but not least, it is beautiful in appearance.

When we learn how other people live, a bond of sympathy and understanding is immediate and they can never again seem completely foreign. The route to understanding is shorter and more sure through food than it is through politics. Some of the answers to understanding the food of the Orient are presented here for the first time in print, as far as I know. The chapters on the philosophy of food present a basic understanding, and in supplying many recipes, the authors have encouraged experimentation.

Vegetables never have been so delicious. Fish and fowl take on new glories. Pork and beef reveal unknown potentials. What is most surprising, all this is possible, for the most part, by using ingredients usually found in American kitchens. Most requirements are found in your local supermarkets. You will learn to cook your usual foods in the Chinese manner, and find yourselves experimenting after very little practice. Few of the recipes take more than twenty minutes. Simmering takes over an hour, but needs no watching. Preparation of the ingredients takes longer than is usual with Western foods, but cooking time is much less.

I envy you who are beginning this adventure—delightful surprises, new combinations, and the fun of preparing them lie just around the corner. There *is* no mystery of the Orient; all is as clear as daylight and is set down here in black and white.

JOHN ASHBY CONWAY

Contents

Introduction

China is a country where the appreciation of good food has been developed into a fine art. International gourmets who have studied the food of all the nations of the world agree that Chinese food has reached a celestial perfection which can delight even the most discriminating taste. The philosophy of the art lies in the secrets of judicious blending and harmonizing of food materials in order to create the most desirable taste.

Unfortunately, Chinese cooking is a closed book to most Western peoples. Among the precious heritages of China which were passed on to the West, her culinary art is the least understood. Thus, this book was written for Americans who want the essence of what Chinese food has to offer and yet are unable to devote long hours to complicated cooking procedures.

The Fine Art of Chinese Cooking is the result of the work of the Academy of the Oriental Arts in Seattle, Washington. This school was founded by the leaders of the Seattle community for the purpose of developing better understanding between the peoples of America and of the Orient. Many courses in Oriental art and philosophy are offered along with the course in Chinese culinary art which my wife May Lee has been teaching for the past five years. Hundreds of American students of the course have been able to prepare authentic Chinese dishes after very few lessons. They learn not only the techniques of food preparation but also the philosophy and logic which are the bases for the traditional Chinese cooking methods.

It is hoped that the readers of this book will, like the students in our classes, learn not only *how* a dish is prepared, but *why*. Once the fundamental principles of the Chinese culinary art are mastered, anyone can cook with intelligence and inspiration. For those

11

who are interested in health, the enjoyment of life, and domestic happiness, *The Fine Art of Chinese Cooking* should have great appeal.

Every attempt has been made to make this book concise, simple, and practical, and to avoid unnecessary jargon and ambiguity. The recipes which have been gathered over many years in China have been put to the practical test in the workshops of the YWCA and the Academy of Oriental Arts. All of the recipes have been selected for their simplicity, practicability, and economy. Almost all of the ingredients can be found in the corner grocery store or at the supermarket. The utensils required are, for the most part, found in the average American kitchen.

Four main groups of foods are given: the first is a collection of authentic Chinese dishes gathered from the different provinces of China; the second is Chinese foods with an American touch, the foods which Americans have already learned to enjoy; the third main group is American food with a Chinese touch, the kinds of dishes which American missionaries and diplomats developed in China; the fourth main group consists of recipes for leftovers and will be of special interest to the homemaker.

For gourmets, connoisseurs, and those who like to take adventures, there is a chapter on Chinese specialties and the great banquet dishes. Special attention is given to vegetables, since the Chinese are regarded as masters of the art of vegetable cooking. The Chinese have many delightful salads which are almost unknown in the West and a chapter is devoted to these. And, of course, there is a chapter on tea.

This book is divided into three main sections.

In Part I, the reader studies the history and philosophy of the Chinese culinary art and learns about the importance of food in the Oriental scale of values. The habits and tastes of the Chinese gourmet and the fundamental principles of the Chinese cookery are explained. Nutritionists will be especially interested in the chapter on Chinese nutritional science.

In Part II, the reader studies the practical science of Chinese cooking and learns of the logic and common sense which are the basis of the traditional cooking methods. There are also practical tips for menu planning, buying, and serving.

Part III is devoted to recipes. The reader is now ready to experiment with various dishes. She will learn very quickly since she knows what she is doing.

Once our readers have acquired a proficiency in the art of Chinese cooking, they will be able to ring the changes on the family diet which, like a change of air, can be only beneficial to the health and happiness.

LEE SU JAN

CHAPTER 1

Confucius, Taoism, and Nutrition

CONFUCIUS: SCHOLAR AND GOURMET

SINCE the earliest stages of Chinese history, food has been a major preoccupation of philosophers and kings. For thousands of years, Chinese scholars have been thinking, talking, and writing about food. It is interesting to compare the traditional Chinese attitude toward food with that of the English, where the art of the table has never been considered part of the intellectual and philosophic life: can one imagine a Thackeray or a Dickens writing a cookbook? In China, however, food is one of the traditional themes of literature, and the most distinguished scholars have always composed recipes, written treatises, and compiled encyclopedias on the culinary arts.

According to Chinese tradition, it was the Emperor Fu Hsi who, in the legendary period more than twenty centuries before the birth of Christ, taught the people how to hunt, fish, cultivate the land, and cook their own food. Cooking could not be considered an art, however, until the Chou Dynasty, the great Classical Age of China (1122-249 B.C.). There is a marked similarity between this era and the great Philosophic Age of Greece: both periods were characterized by social unrest and intellectual ferment. Men, troubled by the state of their world, were moved to thought. The two ages were unusually rich in philosophy and produced systems of thought that covered the range of human opinion. In China, the two dominant philosophies were Confucianism and Taoism: they had a profound effect on the course of Chinese history and influenced every phase of Chinese life, including the culinary arts. Taoism, as we will explain later, was the school which developed

14

the hygienic foods and nutritional science of China. Confucianism concerned itself primarily with the art of cooking.

Confucianism placed a great deal of emphasis on the civilized enjoyment of life and provided a favorable atmosphere for the cultivation of the culinary arts. Only in a society where men of learning are seriously interested in food and where food is appreciated and discussed at distinguished gatherings can eating be elevated from a necessity to an art.

In the Confucian design, the culinary arts were woven into the fabric of the Chinese social order. Confucius stressed social ritual as a teacher of virtue. The feast, where men shared the enjoyment of good foods and celebrated their harmony, constituted an essential part of the Confucian system. Weddings, funerals, birthdays, holidays, public ceremonies were celebrated with appropriate feasting. In the Chinese mind, food and friendship are inseparable, and any gathering without food is considered incomplete and improper. In former days, the temple ritual was celebrated with a feast. It is interesting to compare these Chinese customs with the Jewish ritual dinner of Passover or the agape—love feast—of the early Christians. For the Chinese, the sharing of food at the ceremonial feasts had an almost sacramental character and was an outward sign of the inner harmony and unity of the Chinese social order.

Confucius himself loved good food, and what is more important than loving it, he respected it. It was Confucius who set the standard of culinary correctness and who regulated the custom and etiquette of the table. In the *Analects*, the Chinese are told of many rules which Confucius laid down in regard to the preparation of food. He would not eat when food was stale or without taste, or when improperly blended. His rice had to be polished white; his meat had to be finely minced, properly marinated, and served with the right sauce. He would not use wine or dried meat from the market. If the table were not set correctly and the food served properly, he would not eat.

Who was this Confucius who formed the tastes and regulated the manners of more than one hundred generations of Chinese? Why did Confucianism thrive while other philosophies of the era died? The Chinese are a practical and realistic people who are not easily persuaded by every wandering philosopher. With this cast of mind, they will crush any philosophy which does not square with human nature, and any fantastic ideas, extreme theories of logic, impractical idealism, or excessive abstraction will be instantly rejected. China is a great burial ground of fanatic philosophies.

It was the common sense of Confucius that captured the minds of the Chinese people, and the integrity of his character that won their hearts. They revered him as a man of wisdom and mellowed experience who could teach them how to live because he lived well himself. Moreover, he was a man of impressive scholarship; no man in all China could match him in range and depth of learning. The Chinese are conservative people; they have always respected age, experience, and tradition. Confucius spoke to them from his vast knowledge of Chinese history and tradition and the collective experience of the past, and his philosophy became the mold of the race.

Confucius taught men to be true to their own nature and to live as men, not as animals or angels. At the time in which he lived, China was divided into rival feudal kingdoms; the Emperor was a figurehead, and the harmony of Chinese society was being disrupted by the ambitions and desires of uncultivated men. Confucius realized that there can be no domestic tranquility or peace in society without harmony among men; there can be no peace and harmony among men if they do not have a common interest. He understood human nature too well to think that he could teach men to do what they did not want to do: human nature can be educated, but it can not be stifled. His system of education is based on the refinement and cultivation of men's tastes. For the discord of barbaric pleasures, he substituted the harmony of civilized enjoyments. He taught men that they should live for the enjoyment of simple life, beauty of nature, friendship, art, food, social festivities, family life—all the gentle and beautiful things that contribute to the peace and harmony of society. He taught people to abandon the vanity of ambition, excess, and pride, and to establish a scale of perfection.

His system was based on the concept of the true Chinese gentleman, an ideal that was so fascinating to the Chinese that it has set the seal on their character for over two thousand years. The Chinese gentleman, according to Confucius, was a man of refinement, but not a snob or a sissy; he felt at home in society, but wealth or power did not particularly impress him; he was a scholar, but not a grind—he loved learning but he loved life more; a man of strong inner discipline, but not ascetic. The ideal gentleman of Confucius was a connoisseur, a man who cultivated not only his mind but also his heart and his senses. To Confucius, the man who fed his intellect at the expense of his other faculties had made a bad bargain with life.

Confucius taught his disciples to cultivate artistic living, including the taste for fine food. For thousands of years, therefore, Chinese scholars have been gourmets. When they gather together, usually over an excellent dinner, they talk about food. It is, in fact, their favorite topic of conversation.

In their table conversation, the Chinese gentlemen observe the usual taboos against religion and politics, but for different reasons than do the people in the West. George Bernard Shaw once remarked that religion, politics, and sex were the only topics of interest to the intelligent man. In the West, there is such a variety of religious and political opinion and such fiery devotion to one's own views that custom has dictated the wisdom of talking about less controversial subjects. In the Chinese mind, however, these topics are not considered interesting matter for conversation: politics is considered dirty, and, therefore, beneath a true gentleman's interest; religion, on the other hand, rises above one's knowledge. Confucius himself preferred to treat the mysteries of religion with a respectful silence; in the absence of a direct revelation from heaven, he declined to speculate on the subject. These topics, then, do not interest the Chinese, make no sense to them, and, indeed, make them uncomfortable. The Chinese prefer to discuss the reality of life in which food occupies the first place.

In talking about food intelligently, in analyzing and appraising various dishes, the Chinese scholars created one of the indispensable conditions for the development of any art—an appreciative and discriminating following. The Chinese gourmets have encouraged their chefs to give their best. They have criticized with intelligence, praised with authority, rewarded performance, and crushed incompetence with cold looks more withering than anger.

According to the canons of Confucius, a gentleman was not to venture into the kitchen since that was the province of the master chef. The gourmet and the chef worked together in the manner of a composer and a great violinist, or an architect and a master craftsman. The gourmet would compose the recipe as if it were a poem, turning it in his mind and playing with flavor and texture, color and aroma, as a painter with light and shade, color and form. The recipe was usually quite vague and left vast spaces for the creativity of the chef.

You may be curious about the role of the ladies in the culinary arts. In old China, the ladies from well-to-do families devoted most of their time to bringing up their children and managing their households. They acted as hostesses for the other ladies, since the men and women ate separately. There were servants to prepare food and arrange the tables. If the wife were a gourmet, she helped her husband instruct the head cook.

In modest homes, the wife who cooked well was considered a pearl of great price. She was valued more for her culinary skill than for her beauty—beauty fades, but a good cook improves with age. Her husband would never think of leaving her, since he couldn't bear the prospect of a future without her food. He would brag about her cooking skill to his friends and bring them home to taste her specialties. She could compose a tasty dish from the most humble ingredients.

Many of the delicious dishes of China, like those of France, are of humble peasant origin. The good wife was brought up to be a joy to her husband and her family. Of her many graces, it was her culinary skill which made the greatest contribution to the household. She was the peacemaker. In most instances, the husband's anger could be silenced with an offering of good food. In her hands rested the happiness and health of her family.

The Chinese philosophy considers cooking an art rather than a craft: the gourmet and the chef are not tied to the material but feel free to compose new and original works. In Chinese cooking, the idea and the vision inspiring the dish are important, not the ingredients. The taste of the cooking depends on the *relationship* between the various ingredients and condiments rather than on the *character* of the individual elements. An old Chinese proverb tells us that, if one hopes to become a good cook, he must first become a good matchmaker: the flavors of the ingredients must be "married" and harmonized. Without harmony, there is no taste. It is *harmony* which is the central principle of the culinary arts, the cornerstone of Confucius' teaching, and the central idea of all Chinese philosophy and art. It is, indeed, the *ideal* life of the Chinese people, the lordly, all-pervasive principle before which all lesser principles must bow.

Such a philosophy elevated cooking from a menial and repetitive task to the status of an art. The exquisite, imaginative, and marvelously varied cuisine of China bears a tribute to a philosophy of life that enriched and enobled every facet of man's existence.

TAOISM AND THE SEARCH FOR LONGEVITY

Gourmets of the West are often curious about the fact that the Chinese seem to thrive on this constant feasting. They wonder why the Chinese do not run to fat or drop from apoplexy—after all, the Western world has read the lessons of ancient Rome and those of contemporary insurance statistics. The really dedicated French gourmets are often of elephantine proportions; therefore, it is something of a surprise to find the comparatively sylphlike Chinese gourmet feasting happily into his seventh decade, eyes bright, hair black, teeth intact.

The search for longevity has always been a subject of continuous interest for the Chinese. They have always placed great value on living to a vigorous old age. From the earliest stages of their history, they have been keenly interested in the relationship between food and health. An old Chinese proverb says that all man's diseases enter his mouth and all of his mistakes fly out of it. According to Chinese tradition, it was the great Emperor, Shen Nunn (2737-2697 B.C.) in the legendary period, who discovered the medicinal herbs. He also invented the plow and taught the art of agriculture. He taught the people that they should eat whatever is beneficial to health.

"A healthy mind in a healthy body" could well be a Chinese maxim: what the ancient people of the West accomplished with exercise, the Chinese have achieved with nutrition. The Chinese do not make so strong a distinction between the mental, the spiritual, and the physical as do the people of the West. They consider the mind and the body as a whole, a continuum in which each part gradually shades off into the other; mind and body intermingle and form the whole personality. Because of this attitude toward human nature, Chinese philosophy often contains systems of mental and physical hygiene.

Taoism is the philosophy primarily responsible for the development of hygienic foods. The "nourishment of body and happiness of life" and the search for longevity were one of the principal objects of this philosophy. Taoists were not seeking immortality, as some scholars have erroneously concluded, but were interested in earthly perfection. Whereas the Confucianists were interested in the material aspects of food—its flavor, texture, and appearance—the Taoists were concerned with the "spiritual" or life-giving attributes of various foods.

Taoism is the great counterweight of Confucianism in Chinese philosophy. Its founder, Lao-Tze, the Old Fellow, was a contemporary of Confucius. His answer to the chaos of the times was a return to nature: if man could learn to enjoy the life of simplicity in harmony with nature, he would find integrity, peace, and happiness.

Confucianism was too material, too correct, too grounded in common sense to satisfy the Chinese soul completely; it left no room for the imagination, for the playful spirit, for the desire for freedom beyond the confines of human society. Taoism is a romantic philosophy in contrast to the classical school of Confucius.

The Taoist ideal was a life of simplicity. Lao-Tze believed that man could find health as well as spiritual harmony in nature. He believed that the secret of longevity could be found in plants, the foods closest to nature. With endless patience, the Chinese explored the natural world for young and tender plants, roots, herbs, sea and river vegetation, mushrooms, and seeds in order to find the life-giving elements they were seeking. Through trial and error, they made many important discoveries which are now considered sound doctrine by modern scientists, for in the absence of research laboratories they developed a diet so well-balanced and rich in nutritional value that many modern nutritionists consider it the diet of the future. They realized that the vitality of vegetables could be destroyed by improper cooking, and they emphasized the nutritional superiority of raw or partially cooked vegetables. One might call the Taoists the originators of the salad.

The Chinese have also believed in the nutritional superiority of glandular meats such as heart, liver, and kidney. In China, these foods commanded a higher price than the finest quality muscle meat. Until a generation ago, it was the custom in the United States for butchers to save liver for their customers' cats. Needless to say, the cats thrived. After the medical profession began to emphasize the nutritional value of these foods, however, liver and bacon became a weekly ritual in the American household. As a result, the cost of liver increased manyfold, but it is a nutritional bargain at any price.

Many Chinese foods serve a dual purpose. For example, ginger, one of the favorite condiments of the Chinese, is also used as a home remedy for colds in place of aspirin, and to soothe upset stomachs. Like most of the medicinal herbs, it is taken in the form of a broth.

Onions are also a favorite food for medicinal purposes. The Chinese believe that onions and garlic have a germicidal effect. Fish and onions always were considered a pair for hygienic as well as gastronomic reasons, since not all the inland waters of China were pure.

Americans are so accustomed to finding their medicines in drugstores that they forget many of the modern drugs (aspirin, quinine, cortisone, tranquilizers) had their origins in herbs and the organs of animals.

In our calorie-conscious times, it is interesting to note the emphasis which Taoism and Buddhism placed on the avoidance of rich, heavy meals. The Chinese eat a low-calorie, low-fat diet, and do not really enjoy oily or overly sweet foods. They delight in light, crisp, and delicate food, and prefer savories to sweets.

Because of its low percentage of animal fats, the Chinese diet is attracting the attention of doctors investigating the relationship between cholesterol and impairment of the circulatory system. The Chinese use poly-unsaturated oils, such as peanut oil or sesame oil, in their cooking instead of butter or hydrogenated oils. Until recently they did not drink milk; cream, butter, and cheese were entirely absent from their diet. Calcium was obtained from other sources.

The Chinese diet may well be the diet of the future, since it is admirably suited for the life in modern industrial nations. The sad fact is that the diet of America and Europe, developed for a strenuous life, does not entirely suit a society where machines do the work. The people of the West find that their caloric requirements diminish, yet their habits and appetites refuse to adjust to the new state of affairs. They have literally outgrown Grandmother's cooking.

The alternative seems to be overweight, which is considered unattractive and suicidal, or a life-time of semistarvation. It is sad to see so many people today on depressing and difficult diets. If the trend continues, it will be impossible to eat a dry biscuit with a clear conscience, and the Western world may become as guilt-ridden about food in the 20th Century as it was about sex in the 19th.

Whereas the Chinese believe that a man with a good appetite is blessed by fortune, many modern writers would have one believe him possessed by the devil.

Chinese food may show us a way out of this unhappy dilemma; nutritious and delectable, it preserves health and gives happiness. The gourmet can save his French food for the special occasion, but eat heartily of Chinese cuisine everyday and not suffer for it.

CHAPTER 2

The Elements of the Art of Chinese Cooking

It has often been said that civilization is the process by which man makes an art of a necessity. "There is no man who does not eat and drink," according to Confucius, "but there are few who can appreciate taste." To the Chinese mind, an educated man is one who has a sense of taste; he must have developed not only his intellect but also his senses. It is foolish to talk of this or that school of art unless one can delight in the color and texture of jade. It is literally senseless to write of rhythm in music if we are not moved by the beauty of a song. Every form of art appeals to one or more of the senses. The essence of the culinary arts cannot be found in this or that technique or ingredient; it lies in the taste of the food. We have emphasized this principle at the risk of appearing simple-minded, but simple we must be if we are to become wise. Before this child-like enjoyment of good food, all theory must bow.

It is the quality of inspirations which we value most in a fine dish, that indefinable quality which elevates cooking from a craft to an art. All the great classic dishes of China result from a creative idea in the mind of a gourmet or a chef. One can delight in the vision, logic, surprise, wit, and subtlety which distinguishes a really inspired dish from a merely competent one.

Although man cannot command inspiration, he can work toward knowledge. In every form of art, the artist must study the nature of of his material and the effect it will have on his audience; the painter must understand not only the character of his pigments but also the manner in which the human eye perceives color. Chinese gourmets

24

have always discussed and analyzed their reactions to various dishes, and have developed an extensive knowledge of the nature of food and the physiology of taste.

Many elements enter into our experience of taste. The most important ones are flavor, aroma, texture, and color.

Out of thousands of subtle taste experiences, the Chinese have isolated five primary flavors: sour, pungent, bitter, sweet, and salty. The Chinese have worked with these flavors in various combinations for thousands of years and have learned how they act on each other. Sweet and sour make an interesting pair, for example, whereas sour and salty tend to cancel each other. As do the colors in a color wheel, each flavor has its complementary flavor and its opposite.

The aroma of the food is the second essential element in the taste experience and is almost as important as flavor. We are all aware of how much of the taste of food is lost when we have colds. Many of the subtle tastes of foods are actually fragrances. Many a fragrant food, such as crab, wouldn't be worth eating if we were unable to savor the aroma.

The third characteristic which contributes to our sense of taste is texture. Chinese cooks are almost unsurpassed in their ability to handle this property. The Chinese love sauces of exquisite smoothness, tender-crisp vegetables, and fish which is crisp and crackling on the outside and tender and delicate inside. The great emphasis on texture distinguishes Chinese cuisine from that of Europe; the Chinese gourmet is very much aware of the effect of elastic or crisp textures on the teeth. A fine dish must have one or more of the following textural qualities: softness, fine texture, smoothness, tenderness, crispness. Many Chinese delicacies such as shark fins, bird's nest, and silver fungus are tasteless, colorless, and odorless. They are valued for their interesting texture and purity. Americans, for instance, have learned to like the pleasing crunch of the tasteless water chestnut which absorbs the flavor of the rich primary stock. If one can imagine celery with the texture of noodles, or steak with the consistency of mashed potatoes, he can see how much the quality of taste experience depends on texture.

While color does not have a direct influence on the physiology of taste, it has a very strong influence on the psychological reaction to certain foods. If a strange light were thrown over the dining table so that all the foods looked muddy-green, most people would have a difficult time eating even the most delicious foods. The Chinese arrange the color of the foods on the table as if painting a picture. They delight in the pure whiteness of rice, the delicate greens of baby vegetables, the clear golden tone of rich chicken broth. They will often use green, yellow, and red as an appetizing combination. Sweet-Sour Fish, which is golden brown on the outside and white on the inside, is garnished with green pepper.

The atmosphere of the room, the color and quality of the dishes, and the arrangement of the table enhance our appreciation of food. In the *Analects,* we are told that Confucius would not sit down to eat if the table were not set properly.

Chinese foods often have poetic names which please the ear and linger in the memory. One wonders if the dish called "coral and jade" would taste as sweet if it were simply given its descriptive name: "crab and spinach."

The one unforgivable culinary sin, in the eyes of the Chinese, is monotony. In the matter of food, they are more easily bored than the people of the West, and like to dart from one dish to another. A Western gourmet would regard a sixteen-course dinner as something of a phenomenon, whereas it is only a modest affair to the Chinese. The great and, indeed, infinite, variety of Chinese dishes can be confusing if one does not understand the simple basic principles which have produced them.

In order to simplify the matter, Chinese cooking can be divided into three main orders:

The first order consists of foods which are served in their un-adulterated state with only a touch of garlic, soy sauce, or some other condiment to enhance the natural taste. Most of the classic American dishes, such as steak, fried chicken, and Maine lobster, are of this kind. The art of cooking this kind of food lies in not torturing the material; it is the ingredient itself which carries the day. Some examples of simple Chinese dishes are the barbecued lamb of the Mohammedan tribes and the freshwater crab which is eaten *solus* at an informal claw-probing get-together reminiscent of the Down-East lobster feasts in Maine.

The second order of dishes is more difficult to define. There is still one main ingredient, but it has been changed into the creation of the cook through the alchemy of condiments, sauces, and cooking methods. Most of the classic French dishes as well as many of the great Chinese dishes like Sweet-Sour Fish and Peking Duck are of this kind. Both the Chinese and the French use sauces and condiments superbly to create new dishes. A distinguished sauce is the mark of French cookery, whereas Chinese cuisine is characterized by its condiments. The list of Chinese condiments is almost endless; it includes all those used in the West, plus an exotic array of spices which are used only in Chinese cooking. The main condiments are soy sauce, sesame oil, wine, garlic, scallions, and ginger.

The third and most characteristic order of Chinese dishes is comprised of two or more main ingredients and several condiments living together in perfect accord. In the process of cooking, the elements have undergone complete transfiguration; the dish is not merely a construction, but a new creation.

Harmony, contrast and accent are the three principles of the culinary arts. Harmony, as we have said, is the central, lordly principle of the art of cooking, as well as of all the arts and sciences of China. The art of Chinese cooking lies in the selection, blending and harmonizing of texture, color, aroma, and taste.

The second principle, which is subsidiary to harmony, is contrast; harmony can only exist between things which are not identical. A chord must contain different musical notes, or there is no harmony. If we consider the contrast of color in painting, the thrust and counter-thrust of forces in architecture we can see that contrast is an essential principle in every form of art. The Chinese feast is a study in contrast; sweets are played against salts, smoothness against crunchiness, large foods against miniature ones, hot foods against cold ones.

The third aesthetic principle is accent, or dominance. The Chinese do not believe in saying too many things at the same time. Every work of art must make a statement; accent within a dish means that there must be one harmonized theme in a dish, not a confusion of conflicting elements. In dishes which combine meat and vegetables, for example, the meat usually dominates the vegetables.

The actual cooking methods of the Chinese are not greatly different from those which are used in the West. The Chinese also simmer, sauté, deep fry, marinate, and so forth, as you will see. There are three essential distinctions between Chinese cooking methods and those of the West, however, which must be emphasized. Cutting is one of the most important techniques in Chinese cooking, whereas it is only of minor importance in the West. Cutting is a very important step in preparing harmonic dishes; you can combine all kinds of dissimilar ingredients, or at least make a good try, as long as they are cut in a uniform size and a harmonious shape.

The second basic difference is one which we have already mentioned, the greater emphasis on condiments in China than in the West.

The third difference between Chinese and Western cooking lies in the manner of preparation. Chinese dishes require a maximum of preparation and a minimum of cooking, while in the West the converse is true.

Up to a certain point, the quality of the cuisine improves with the development of a civilization. The author has eaten with primitive tribes many times and found their cooking to be as unsophisticated as their culture. After a society reaches dizzying technological heights, however, the quality of the culinary arts often goes into a decline. People become a part of the machine, and they do not take time to eat properly. This is true in Communist China today; the energies of the people are being consumed in the drive toward material progress and there is no time for the cultivation of the old art of living. In the days before the revolution the role of the culinary arts vis-à-vis the level of progress was the exact opposite of what is in

China today. Although many of the arts and sciences had become stagnant, the culinary arts had continued to develop. In the old days a traveler returning to China after an absence of several years would be amazed at the number of new ideas in the art of making food.

The West judges men and nations by their works, while the Oriental people have always judged them by their tastes. The Chinese do not take the measure of the man by what he does for a living as much as by the things which make him enjoy living. Their ancient philosophies have taught them that the purpose of living is the enjoyment of the simple life. Although the Oriental people have not made so much material progress as the people of the West, they have learned how to enjoy what they have. Rich or poor they are happy for the roofs over their heads and a good meal with friends in the evening. Oriental philosophy has always emphasized the humanistic science, whereas the West, during the past three hundred years, has made great strides in the physical sciences. The people of the West have produced many wonderful things, but they are losing the capacity to enjoy them.

CUISINE OF THE DIFFERENT SCHOOLS

Although the fundamental principles of the culinary arts were observed in all of China, there was a variation in the food of the different provinces. Because of the antiquated transportation facilities, each area developed its own style of eating and its own specialties. A Chinese is most partisan about the food of his own province; the easiest way to draw him into a heated argument is to imply that the food of the neighboring province is superior to that of his own. The man from Canton will yield to no man, and neither will the native of Peking or Foochow. The delightful regional variations in the cuisine of China are an embarrassment of riches from the standpoint of the poor scholar. How can one enumerate all the fine dishes which can be found in every province? We can, however, briefly describe five provincial schools which are especially noted for their contributions to the Chinese culinary art: they are the schools of Honan, of Peking, of Canton, of Foochow, and of Szechwan.

Honan is the ancient cultural center of China. It lies on the Yellow River, which, like the Tigris-Euphrates and the Nile, was a cradle of ancient civilization. This school is especially known for its sweet-sour dishes; the carp from the Yellow River is one of the delicacies of this area, its most famous recipe being Sweet-Sour Fish.

Peking is the intellectual and cultural center of modern China; it has been the seat of government since the 12th Century. It lies in the gateway between China and the barbarian world, in sight of the Great Wall. Peking, "the City of the North," has been occupied many times by barbarians and has succeeded again and again in vanquishing her conquerors. Shaggy warriors have roared through her gates only to be transformed into Chinese gentlemen a generation later. A city of paradox, it was laid out in a majestic style by Kublai Khan, the great Mongolian conqueror who became the patron of all things Chinese. It contains within itself the finest of Chinese culture as well as the colorful, primitive world of the Asian plains.

For centuries many of the finest chefs of the various provinces migrated to Peking and established restaurants, specializing in the food of their own province. The traveler who wandered through the streets of Peking could discover the taste of the finest from every province of China.

On the street of Si Chang An Chieh there were ten famous restaurants, each with its own special taste, yet all claiming to be from the province of Szechwan. Outside Chienmen there were several restaurants noted for the most famous specialty of the area, the authentic Peking Duck.

Many of the famous restaurants had used the same stoves for centuries and valued them in the same manner in which a fine vintner holds on to his old casks. There was one Mohammedan restaurant which specialized in Flavor Roast Lamb,* cooked on a stove which had been in its possession since the Ming Dynasty.

---

* See recipe in the chapter on Classic Chinese Foods.

This restaurant was also known for its sauce, a recipe as old as the stove. For four hundred years its pure and heavenly fragrance filled the air for four blocks.

Among the people of Peking, there was a saying that men and food must come to the city to be "renovated." Country boys and country dishes were polished and given a certain grandeur after they passed through the gates of Peking. There were adventurers and gourmets in that city who had the money and the leisure to cultivate a connoisseur's taste.

The first group was the Manchus, the Imperial Family before the establishment of the Republic of China. As their name implies, they were originally from Manchuria. They conquered China, estab-their seat at Peking, aand became patrons of Chinese culture, including the culinary arts. Their style of cuisine was known as Imperial Food. They had a gargantuan three-day feast or banquet known as the Manchu Feast.

The Salt Monopolists were another group of gourmets from Peking. They held a hereditary monopoly on the production of salt and were richer than most of the ruling classes. They were untroubled by antitrust laws, competition, or the necessity to improve their product. They already had their palaces, and the form of conspicuous consumption which most interested them was food.

The third group was the bankers. The exterior of a Chinese bank was as sober and conservative as that of its Western counterpart. The interior, however, was more like the palaces of European feudal lords. Diamonds, pearls, precious jade, works of art, and other treasures could be found there, because a bank was a mint, jewelry shop, trading monopoly, art dealer, pawn shop, insurance company, and real estate firm as well as a commercial savings and trust institution. The banks tended to cluster around Peking, since the government lived on borrowed money. The bankers themselves were a princely lot who lived in the style of the merchant families of the Italian Renaissance. They kept short hours and devoted themselves to good wine, entertainments, and wild parties.

The school of *Shantung* is almost indistinguishable from that of

Peking. For centuries the two areas have been exchanging chefs. The cooks of Shantung Province brought the food of their province to the capital city, and cooks from the city came to Shantung and opened restaurants in the style of Peking.

Canton is the principal city of Kwangtung Province and was the gateway to the West when the European powers began to trade with the Orient. It is a seaport, an ancient trading city which has always looked to the outside world, whereas most of China, as an agricultural country, has tended to look to itself. The name "Cantonese" has attached itself to the food of the entire province; the best Cantonese food was not from the city, however, but from the country districts of Tailiang in the district of Shun Teh. For centuries, the people from Tailiang have been epicureans, and are noted for their ability to invent novel delicacies. They are the originators of fried milk—a kind of cheese—and are also noted for their turtle soup, sausages, oyster stew, and wild pheasant rolls.

Foochow is the neighbor of Kwangtung and is also a seafaring province. The cooking of Canton and Foochow, however, is very different in character. The province has a long coastline and is noted for its fine sea food. Pork Velour is another most delightful dish from Foochow, and their Red Fermented Bean Sauce was highly regarded throughout China.

Szechwan in the southwest of China has two styles of cuisine. The native food of the province contains a great number of hot pepper dishes. In the early Ch'ing Dynasty (17th Century), however, large numbers of people from Peking migrated to this area, and the people adopted the style of Peking for their formal banquets, when hot, spicy dishes are not served. One of the great favorites is Szechwan Duck, a version of Peking Duck which equals if not excels the original.

How to be a Gourmet

The reader is probably wondering which of the main schools of Chinese cuisine is the best. It is a difficult decision to make, since they all have their charms, and certain gourmets prefer one school and others prefer another. There is, however, a fairly constant standard by which Chinese gourmets judge food, whether it be from Canton or Honan. The following criteria can be used to take the measure of any Chinese food. In order to pass the test, the food should have one or more of the following qualities:

Pure: the equivalent of the Western idea of clear and concentrated, as in rich, clear, chicken stock. Weak, insipid, or muddy broths and gravies do not qualify.

Sweet: Not sugar-sweet, but that indefinable quality which we refer to when we speak of sweet air or sweet water.

Smooth: the quality which is usually achieved by the proper use of cornstarch. Anything lumpy or bumpy, any pastiness in a sauce will disqualify a dish.

Young and *Tender:* the qualities of young vegetables. Tough, overgrown, or mushy vegetables are to be avoided.

Texture: the dish should have one or more of several textures—crispness, tenderness, smoothness, softness. The textures to be avoided are sogginess, stringiness, or mushiness. Texture is a matter of integrity. If a dish is supposed to be crisp, let it be crisp; if it is to be tender, let it melt in your mouth.

Color: also a matter of integrity. If the vegetables are cooked properly they will be clear green, not olive green. A sauce should have some character; it should be a rich brown, or light and clear in tone. A rich, pure broth has a clear, golden hue.

THE MIRACLE OF TEA

The cult of tea drinking is an integral part of the Chinese gourmet's experience. Tea is the child of Taoism. It leads into a world of quiet contemplation of the simple beauties of life. One drinks tea in order to leave behind all worldly concerns and to enter into the moment of sanity. Luxury, pomp, ambition, and ostentation have no place in the drinking of tea. It is not for those who wear silk pajamas and eat rich food. It is only for those who understand the Taoist maxim: naturalness is beauty, simplicity is truth.

The Chinese savors the color and aroma of fine tea and cele-brates the seasons: spring, and the flowering of a favorite tree; autumn, and the falling of the leaves in the garden.

Lovers of tea regard its preparation as a special enjoyment. Dev-otees of the cult of tea use waters from mountain streams and serve the tea from rare cups. Many years ago on a visit to the sum-mer palace of the Imperial Family, the author saw the marble ves-sels which the ladies in waiting would set out in the garden to capture dew for infusing the Dowager Empress' tea.

The famous tea ceremony one hears about is a creation of Zen Buddhist monks; its purpose is to teach one to discover serenity and beauty in the simple things of life. In keeping with the Zen idea of simplicity, the vessels are humble, the tearoom plain and bare. The ceremony of preparing and drinking tea is highly stylized and is observed in silence.

The Chinese connoisseur of tea is very much like the European student of wine; he can tell the life history of tea from a sip and is very fond of sniffing, savoring, and talking about tea. Tea and wine can be expensive fields of study. There are teas in Hong Kong which sell for ten cents a pound—and there are those which sell for three hundred dollars a pound. There is a tea which is truly worth its weight in gold: one ounce of tea for one ounce of gold.

Although the Chinese are very sane in regard to wine, they are completely mad about tea. They became such connoisseurs that they began to demand better and better and better tea. In certain areas of China, men have ruined themselves for the precious stuff. In this area of Chinese life we can say that the Confucian canon of moderation was honored more in the breach than in the observance.

Fine tea is clear and pale gold in color; it has a natural sweetness and does not need any sugar, milk, or lemon. In fact, any adulter-ants would be a sacrilege. Good tea is not brisk. There is no taste of bitterness in a fine tea; it does not leave a fur on the tongue. The bouquet is exquisite, and there is a long persistent "back flavor" which connoisseurs consider the mark of a superior tea. Bad tea is either too light or too dark, and it has a bitter, crude taste which must be obliterated with sugar and lemon.

There are three kinds of teas: green, red, and black. The green teas are usually better than the red teas, and the red teas outrank the black teas. There are many exceptions to this hierarchy, however; each group has its own merit, its own fine teas, and its own following. A really fine black tea may outrank a so-so green tea. The famous Goddess of Mercy tea combines the best qualities of green, red, and black teas. Green teas are made from young tender leaves which are baked as soon as they are picked. The red and black teas are allowed to pass through a period of fermentation before they are softened and fired; the main difference between red and black tea is that the black is from more mature leaves. Tea is sold whole leaf and broken leaf. The whole leaf is superior to the broken leaf, because the second is made from large and often bitter leaves. Whole-leaf tea is made from tiny, medium, or large leaves, and the quality as well as the price is in an inverse ratio to the size of the leaves. The tiny, whole leaves are very fine and have no bitterness; they were picked before the tannic acid had begun to take over the flavor. The worst of all possible teas is brick tea, which is sold to the Mongols. The tea is actually baked in bricks which are as hard as concrete. It is vile.

The character of a tea as well as that of a wine is created by the place where it was grown and the place where it was processed. The flavor cannot be exactly duplicated elsewhere.

The really superb teas are hoarded like vintage port or fine old brandy. They are saved for special occasions and are served with calculated modesty. "Oh, it is nothing really. Just a little tea," the host says as he watches the guests to see if they really know what they are drinking. The Goddess of Mercy and the finest types of precious teas are served alone, since food would obliterate the delicate flavors. The really fine teas are complex and subtle in contrast to the simple and open everyday teas.

In the old days, tea was forbidden on the table during meals.

The connoisseur felt it was meant to be served after meals, when it could be enjoyed without distraction. In recent years, however, because of the Western influence, it has become acceptable to serve tea with meals.

Today the role of the cup of tea on the Chinese table is similar to the American water goblet and the European glass of wine. Tea is the only drink which satisfies the Chinese thirst.

Teas for the table are rather like the everyday table wines of Europe. They are of good rather than spectacular quality. Freshness, purity, and lightness are the qualities valued in a table tea. Tea is much more delicate in flavor than wine and plays a more retiring role on the table. A good table tea harmonizes unobtrusively with flavors of the food, cools and refreshes the palate, and aids the digestion. Bitter tea spoils the taste of food.

Three types of tea can be served with meals. Although the teas are sometimes associated with different kinds of food, there are no strict rules governing the matter.

Kind	Qualities	May be served with:
Green Tea	cooling, refreshing, clean in flavor, aids digestion	highly flavored foods, fried dishes
Jasmine Tea (green tea with flowers, Formosa type)	fragrant, delicate, romantic	rich foods, oily foods
Red Tea	pleasing color, full-bodied flavor, warming rather than cooling	associated especially with sea food, which is considered a "cold" food

Tea has served the Chinese people well for over a thousand years. The boiling of water for tea may very well be credited with the survival of the race—the Chinese never drank water because the water was not fit to drink. Tea is the most innocent of life's pleasures. It is a social lubricant more wholesome than liquor, a psychological comforter which refreshes and does not destroy. In a violent world, tea restores the mind and provides an island of peace for the soul. With his pot of tea, the exiled Chinese is at home anywhere in the world.

Rules for making good tea

1. The first rule is to buy good tea. Making tea is very simple, and the end product is never any better than the material—and seldom worse, as is often the case with coffee.

2. The tea leaves are put in the cup or pot of china or glass. Metal should not come in contact with tea. Use approximately one-half teaspoon per cup. With very good tea you can serve 6 people using only 2 teaspoons.

3. Boil the water, never the tea. The water must be brought to a rolling boil and must be poured over the leaves immediately.

4. Pour the water over the tea leaves. Cover the pot or cup.

5. In a few minutes the tea is ready. Do not cook for a "rich, dark color." Good tea should be pale gold.

6. Everything used in the preparation of tea must be absolutely clean and free of oil.

In the Chinese style, sugar, milk, lemon, or cream is taboo. The best Chinese teas have a natural, sweet flavor and no bitterness. They need no adulterants; most of the tea in the West, however, requires sugar and lemon. The good teas can be infused two times— in fact, the second round is often better than the first. Simply pour the water over the leaves after the pot has been emptied and have some more tea.

CHAPTER 3

Ingredients and Condiments

INGREDIENTS

IN THE long history of their civilization, the Chinese have had many opportunities to experiment with all kinds of foods. The range of ingredients and the variety of their dishes is so vast as to seem almost endless.

China, as an agricultural country, lived at the mercy of the great powers of nature and was subject to the changing moods of great rivers and capricious rains. In times of drought and flood the people would eat anything to stay alive—roots, fungus, strange plants—and in these tragic and desperate times made valuable food discoveries. In China necessity was a powerful incentive to gastronomic courage.

We must not forget, however, the role of prosperity in the progress of the culinary art. There were periods in Chinese life when the rain was benevolent and the rivers gentle, the harvest abundant and the living easy. From their full larders, the Chinese gave feasts to celebrate their good fortune with family and friends. When they feel affluent the Chinese put their money into food rather than into other things. Europeans living in China used to say that the Chinese put all their money in food while the people of the West put theirs into armaments.

The exotic delicacies of China were discovered as often by men who were idle and curious as by those who were poor and desperate. In China there have always been men who have had the wealth and leisure to cultivate a fine palate. To the depths of the Yellow Sea, to the tops of the Himalayan Mountains, almost, indeed, to the ends of the earth, these connoisseurs would send their servants to find the most exotic of foods.

Travelers in China always carried trunks full of delicacies. Sea cucumber, shark's fin, bird's nest, and bear's paw may seem strange and unappetizing things to the Western mind, but they are like manna to the Chinese, and they are more expensive than any Western food with the possible exceptions of Black Sea caviar, and paté de fois gras.

In addition, the Chinese used most of the foods which are part of the Western diet, such as pork, lamb, beef, chicken, duck, fish, shrimps, lobster, and crab. Although the Chinese have many vegetables and fruits which are widely used in the West—potatoes, tomatoes, dry onions, spinach, egg plant, strawberries, lettuce, and celery, to name a few—they have many vegetables and fruits which are not eaten in the West. Some of these include pea vines, bok choy and lichee nuts. There are few Western foods which are not part of the Chinese cuisine.

Since this book is dedicated to the American household, the greater part will be devoted to recipes which use only foods available in the American market. A chapter on specialties, however, contains the classic banquet dishes, such as Peking Duck and Bird's Nest Soup, which we feel will be of special interest to the gourmet; a trip to the Chinese market will be necessary for those who wish to try a hand at preparing these exotic delicacies.

Meat

When the Chinese think of meat, it is usually pork. Beef in China has never been used widely. The Chinese cow is actually a water buffalo and is used in the fields to draw the plow. The economy of agricultural China rested on the back of this strong, patient animal, and the Chinese have never really had the heart to eat it. In the *Analects* we are told that Confucius was greatly distressed to hear the sound of the slaughter of China's best friend and that he felt that it would be generous and merciful to spare the animal after its long years of faithful service. The introduction of Buddhism reinforced the sacrosanct status of the cow. We might also add that retired water buffalo is not exactly like prime Western beef, but the Chinese can make it taste like tenderloin. (Beef is becoming more popular, however, with the increasing contact with the West.)

The pig became the food animal in China because it reproduced in litters and was not useful for field work. Lamb was introduced into the Chinese diet by the Mohammedans who followed the Jewish dietary laws.

The Chinese do not eat as much meat as the Western nations, not only for reasons of economy, but also as a matter of preference. In the Western cuisine there is no food that has so much status or generates so much interest as rare prime beef or a whole leg of lamb. The Chinese, on the other hand, are not really fascinated by great slabs of meat. They prefer a dish in which meat is harmonized with vegetables and other ingredients in an artful way—the meat lending its flavor to the vegetables and receiving in turn a lighter, more varied, and more interesting texture from its partners. Meat alone seems too heavy and greasy to the Chinese. Whenever meat is served, it is usually cut finely or sliced paper thin.

Fowl

The Chinese eat chicken, wild fowl, and duck; one of the most famous of Chinese dishes is the aristocratic Peking Duck in which the duck is force fed in a manner similar to the French method of preparing the goose for *pâté de foie gras*. Chicken is used with ham in the primary soup stock which is the basis of so many Chinese dishes.

Stock

The Chinese put a great deal of time, thought, and money into their soup. It forms the foundation of so many of their dishes. There was a restaurant in Peking, noted for its elegant fare, which had a primary soup stock worth thousands of dollars; thousands of chickens had gone into the cauldron to produce the pure, rich broth which was the basis of the restaurant's specialties and the reason for its distinguished reputation. The authors do not feel that it is worth while for most American families to boil down several pounds of meat to produce a quart of rich stock. In its place we use clear, canned chicken broth, which has a fine rich flavor. Substitutes which may be used in certain dishes are bouillon cubes and powdered chicken stock.

Fish and Sea Food

The Chinese make great use of these foods. China has a long seacoast and her people have explored the ocean depths for such exotic things as sea cucumber, shark's fin, squid, lobster, shrimp, and crab.

The Chinese are in love with fresh-water fish, however, and actually prefer it to sea food. Nothing is more elegant to the Chinese than a fresh fish cooked with understanding. Fish-farming is an ancient and an important part of the Chinese economy. There are many rivers which yield abundant harvests of fish. The carp from the Yellow River is a delicacy which has been appreciated by the Chinese since the beginnings of their civilization. Fresh-water shrimp and crab are valued more than their sea-going counterparts.

In Chinese restaurants fish and sea food are kept alive and swimming in vats until their appointed hour. Such absolutely fresh fish has a wonderfully pure and delicate flavor. In the United States, fish has never found its proper place, although the people are very fond of shrimp, lobster, and various other kinds of seafood. It is our opinion that the reasons for the devaluation of fish in this country is the objection to fishy tastes and odors. Fishiness is partially caused by improper cooking, especially by excessive heat. It may also be caused by a lack of freshness. Even the most exquisitely cared-for fish can become fishy, however, if the proper condiments are not used. In this book we will show you how to purify the flavor and odor of fish through the use of marinades of wine, soy sauce, and onions. One of Mrs. Lee's pupils had a horror of fish in any form; she threatened to leap over the table if we ever dared cook fish in class. Finally we persuaded her to taste our specially prepared fish and she couldn't eat enough of it. She said that it tasted like chicken.

At the present time commercial fisheries in the West are throwing away various kinds of fish which could become valuable foods if they were cooked properly. They are called "trash fish" and are given such unappetizing names as dogfish and bull-head. In the future they may become valuable foods if cooked with understanding, just as liver and kidney, which were thrown away twenty years ago, are now highly regarded by Western gourmets.

Dairy Products

These foods were long notable for their absence from the Chinese diet. The Chinese did not use milk, cheese, yogurt, butter, or anything related to milk—they could not tolerate them. Recently, however, because of the Western influence, they have started to eat these foods, and we will include some new Chinese recipes which use dairy products. Considering the unhygienic conditions in some parts of China, it was as prudent for the Chinese to abstain from dairy products as it was for the Jewish people to abstain from pork.

In place of milk products the Chinese have developed a "bean dairy." The versatile soy bean was made into soy milk, the milk into pudding, cheese, "bean skin," and bean curd.

Vegetables

The Chinese eat large quantities of vegetables, not only for reasons of economy, but also because of their nutritional theories. They believe that vegetables are very superior foods from a health-giving standpoint. Millions of Chinese Buddhists are vegetarians, and many others abstain from meat for reasons of health. The Chinese have developed the art of vegetable cookery to a level which approaches perfection. The most characteristically Chinese dishes are those which harmonize meat and vegetables. The use of the bean in the Chinese diet is almost endless. Soy bean is the thing which keeps the Chinese Buddhists alive and healthy. It is the vegetable which most resembles meat in the quality of its protein.

CONDIMENTS

The Chinese make greater use of condiments than any nation of the West. They use all the spices which are known in Europe and America as well as an exotic array of spices unknown outside of the Orient, such as dry red blossom from Tibet, wild cinnamon, and anise pepper.

It was the lure of spices from the East which established the great trade routes from Europe to India and Cathay and led them to seek a shorter route to the Orient across the waters of the Atlantic.

The use of condiments varies somewhat from province to province. In Canton, for example, the original taste of the food is preferred, and very little wine and soy sauce are used. In Shanghai soy sauce is used, but the food contains almost no garlic.

Condiments are used to enhance the flavors of foods and to suppress any flavors and odors which we would gladly forego. The proper use of condiments can purify the fishiness of fish, the wild taste of game, and the strong taste of certain kinds of liver. Condiments blend the flavors of dissimilar ingredients and form a bond between them.

Garlic

The prince of condiments is used as knowingly in Chinese food as it is in Continental cuisine. Garlic was introduced to Italy by Marco Polo and was then taken up by the French. It has been widely used in the United States during only the past three decades.

Sherry

The Chinese have a very dry yellow wine that is used in cooking and has a flavor very similar to that of sherry. A good dry sherry is an excellent substitute. Sauterne may also be used. The Northern Chinese use a great deal of wine in their cooking. To the American taste, their cuisine tastes very much like French cooking. Abstainers may use wine in cooking with a clear conscience, since the alcohol is completely evaporated in the cooking and only the flavor remains. The Chinese use wine as a marinade. Wine and soy sauce are used to eliminate fishy tastes and the odor of certain meats.

Monosodium Glutamate (MSG)

This is a salt of vegetable protein which heightens the flavor of food. It must be used with discretion since it can wipe out the subtle distinction of a dish if used to excess.

Sesame Oil

A most fragrant and delicious oil made from sesame seeds—wonderful to cook with, but expensive. For reasons of economy one does not deep fry with sesame oil. The Chinese use sesame oil as a condiment in the same way as the French use butter; it is not only a lubricant but also a means of enhancing the flavors of foods and adding a delicate flavor of its own. Peanut oil is a good substitute since it has an agreeable flavor and takes heat well. Any unhydrogenated oil may be used. A few drops of sesame oil in a bottle of peanut oil is an agreeable compromise between flavor and economy. Corn oil and vegetable oil are other choices.

All these oils are poly-unsaturated and, according to contemporary nutritional theory, excellent for the health. Soy oil is in disrepute among the Chinese; it develops a disagreeable flavor when heated and has the reputation of having a disquieting effect on the digestive system. It was used by ordinary Chinese restaurants in China because it was inexpensive.

Soy Sauce

This is a most characteristically Chinese condiment. It enhances the flavors of foods and suppresses any disagreeable qualities. It purifies the taste of fish and liver, adds interest to vegetables, and brings out the flavor of meat. It is readily available in bottles at most grocery markets.

Ginger

Another characteristically Chinese condiment is ginger. Whole, fresh, ginger root is the most desirable, and we are happy to note that it is becoming available on the American market. You might try to plant some ginger in an outdoor herb garden. Dried ginger root and powdered Oriental ginger are substitutes. Powdered ginger is often more convenient in some dishes. We must warn our readers, however, that the taste of ginger is not always agreeable to the Western palate. Children especially dislike it. Use it with discretion and increase the amount gradually until you develop a taste for it. Ginger powder is especially strong, and the reader should be very careful about using it. A "pinch" of ginger powder powder is really too much; a "whiff" might be a better term. Ginger root should be stored in a dry place, *not* in the refrigerator.

Sugar

The Chinese use sugar as a condiment in order to enhance the flavors of foods. Its use varies from province to province. Some areas like to use a great deal of sugar in their cooking, and other areas use only a small amount.

Fortunately most of the condiments which we have listed are available on the American market. Powdered garlic or garlic salt, onion salt, and ginger powder may be kept in reserve on the shelves. Most of the recipes require only these condiments. A few recipes which use Chinese star anise; regular anise is a substitute, and it may be omitted if it is not available in your area.

In addition there are many condiments in the great Chinese market which will be of interest to food hunters. Bottled oyster sauce is of great interest to gourmets, although it is too expensive for everyday use. It is used in place of soy sauce and has an elegant flavor.

A Note on Condiments

The quantities of condiments given in the recipes follow as closely as possible the Chinese standard of taste in order to give our American readers the authentic Chinese flavor. In many cases, however, it has been necessary to subdue the taste somewhat, since the Western palate must learn to accommodate itself to certain

flavors. Some of our readers may still find the quantity of garlic or
soy sauce overwhelming, and we urge them to adjust to measure to
their liking.

If a dish seems too salty, the salt should be reduced or eliminated
before there is any attempt to tamper with the amount of soy sauce
given in the recipe. If the dish is still too salty, the soy sauce may be
gradually reduced.

CHAPTER 4

Menu Planning and Serving

MENUS

A BEAUTIFUL dinner is truly a work of art. The resourceful cook must compose her piece in such a way that it pleases and intrigues her guests and lingers in their memories. The planning of the menu is really one of the most exacting phases of the culinary arts; it involves the selecting, contrasting, and harmonizing of the various dishes, and calls for imagination, judgment and a certain amount of playfulness. If the American housewife finds herself with knotted brow in regard to next week's dinner party, she can console herself with the idea that it is no small challenge, but rather one that has been revolved in the minds of the greatest gourmets and cooks.

Chinese people have solved this dilemma of what to have for dinner by having developed certain traditional rules regarding the combinations of foods, and they have some very distinguished classic menus for every occasion. They are not fettered by these rules however; they serve as an inspiration for the cook.

The traditional Chinese feast is like a stately and impressive procession in which each dish harmonizes and contrasts with the one before and after it as do the movements of a symphony. Harmony, the central principle of the culinary arts, must unite the various dishes; it is a subtle principle and must be felt.

Contrast is the spice of the dinner; it lures the guest on from one dish to the next. The Chinese play with this concept in a deliberate and fanciful manner. After a dry dish, soup will be served; a crunch dish will be served to precede a creamy smooth one; a massive dish such as Peking Duck will be presented with appealing miniature

47

delectables such as snails or baby vegetables. The cook will ring the changes on the basic flavors of the dishes: a pungent dish such as Hot Pepper Beef will be served with a sweet or bland accompaniment. Old flavors such as mushrooms will be served with fresh young flavors like baby peas, or bird's nest. Sweet things are often served between courses to pique the interest and the salty things are served near the end of the meal in order to carry flagging appetites of the guests to the finish line.

The basic aesthetic principle is accent or dominance which means that every kind of art from poetry to dinner parties must make a statement; the dinner must not fly off in all directions at once, but must have a point of focus in a principle dish. Every other dish must be subordinated to this main dish and must harmonize with it. In the long and elaborate Chinese feast, there are many dishes and many minor crescendos, but, nonetheless, the main point is not lost. "What kind of feast did you attend, dear brother," the Chinese scholar will ask his friend. "Shark's Fin," "Peking Duck," "Bird's Nest," or "Sea Cucumber" might be the reply. The main dish tells the tale, not only of the other dishes but also of the cost.

The traditional Chinese feasts are just too complicated for home cooking. When the Chinese who do not have a full staff decide to give a really stunning party, they usually go to restaurants because life is too short to try to manage it at home. There is not much point in giving the readers instruction on preparing the extremely elaborate, complex, and expensive ceremonial meals since the trend today among Chinese gourmets is toward a simpler menu. The gargantuan Manchu feast is extinct, and the other feasts are reserved for a state occasion. While Americans are being influenced by Chinese foods and customs, the Chinese have also been benefited by Western ways which have become incorporated in their style of living. In the old days, for example, the men and the ladies ate separately at fairly large parties. The new way among Chinese gourmets in the West is to have a dinner party for six or eight friends, where husbands and wives sit together. The food is simple but distinctive, and its courses seldom exceed eight. We have included in this chapter menus which exemplify using the Chinese principles of composing a dinner, but which are suitable for American life today. We have, for example, put the sweets at the end of the meal in the American fashion. The reader should feel free to make changes to suit her way of life; if she finds the soup course tedious without serving help, then by all means, omit it. There is no reason why a cook could not combine Chinese food with American or European dishes, as long as she knows what she is doing. A great deal of the food of North China, for example, is reminiscent of the French cuisine and would go well with any French dishes. After a while our students develop a feeling for Chinese food and an intuitive understanding of the fundamental principles of combined foods.

The Chinese believe a good appetite brings happiness and a man blessed with this faculty has been favored by fortune. According to this tradition, the culinary arts have three purposes: first of all to stimulate the appetite through deliciously flavored and attractively served meals; secondly to vary the daily diet, which has a beneficial effect on the health and mental outlook; finally to create domestic happiness through leisurely, happy, and delightful meals which create harmony, banish strife, and heal the wounds of the day's struggle.

A Note on Menu Planning

The banquets which we have planned may be served at a buffet or at dining tables. Cooking a banquet of this kind is quite a production unless kitchen help is hired for the occasion.

The dinner party menus have been planned with the American housewife in mind. They can be cooked and served without serving help. Quick-fried dishes, which must be prepared at the last minute, are combined with *hung-shao* dishes which may be prepared in advance and put in the refrigerator or freezer. Desserts can usually be prepared in advance. The foods may be cleaned and cut and put in refrigerator jars an hour or so before the guests arrive in order to avoid last minute confusion.

The family menus are simple and make use of leftovers and foods which can be cooked in advance. Some of our students like to prepare *hung-shao* dishes for supper while they are cooking lunch. Making double portions of certain dishes is a time-saver. Meatballs, fish, rice, and noodles can be cooked in abundance and banked in the refrigerator for future use.

MENUS

FAMILY MEALS

Celery Salad
Fried Pork with Bamboo Shoots   Plain Rice
Precious Fruit   Hot Tea

Tomato and Onion Salad
Sweet-Sour Spareribs   Fried Rice with Pork
Precious Grapefruit   Tea

Chicken Noodle Soup
Mandarin Fried Shrimp with Water Chestnuts
Plain Rice
Almond Cookies   Tea

DINNER PARTIES

Celery Cabbage and Ham Soup
Savory Pork with Mushrooms
Asparagus   Ten Precious Noodles
Walnut Dates   Tea

Chicken Soup
Savory Beef with Eggs
Fried Pork with Celery Cabbage   Ten Precious Rice
Peking Dust   Tea

Chicken Noodle Soup
Shrimp Omelet
Savory Chicken with Celery Cabbage
Mandarin Fish
Snow Peas   Plain Rice
Almond Tea

Chinese Vegetable Soup
Chicken Chop Suey
Barbecued Spareribs
Crab Omelet
Many Precious Fried Rice
Almond Curd   Tea

BANQUET

This is a Westernized version of the traditional Chinese banquet.

Hors d'Oeuvres
Sliced Cold Savory Roast Beef
Sweet-Sour Celery Salad
Skewered Chicken Livers
Cold Savory Pork with Eggs

Main Course
Sherry Chicken
Mandarin Fried Shrimp with Water Chestnuts
Tempura
Sweet-Sour Spareribs
Ten Precious Fried Rice
Sub Gum Chao Mein
Green Peas with Mushrooms
Zuccini
Almond Tea with Cherries
Tea   Coffee

This banquet menu follows the traditional Chinese pattern with a few modifications.

Hors d'Oeuvres

Canned Abalone, shredded thin without dressing
Preserved Duck Eggs,* cut in six pieces
Cold Savory Pork
Marinated Mushrooms

Soup

Sour and Pungent Soup

Fried Dishes

Walnut Chicken
Butterfly Shrimp
Sub Gum
Green Peas with Mushrooms

Main Course

Sharks' Fins
Sweet-Sour Fish
Savory Pork with Eggs
Peking Duck
Ten Precious Fried Rice
Almond Tea   Tea

A NOTE ABOUT SERVING

Many Chinese gourmets are beginning to have second thoughts about the traditional Chinese manner of serving food. We will depart from the custom of our ancestors and heartily recommend that Americans serve Chinese dishes in the style of the West. According to the usual custom everyone has his own individual bowl of rice, but the dishes in the center of the table belong to the party.

* May be bought in the Chinese market.

Everyone eats directly from the common dishes with his chop sticks. Our Western friends think this is a good way to spread the plague, and they may be right. Chinese foods can be served at the dinner table from platters and plates, with serving spoons and individual plates, in a modified Chinese fashion; or they can be served in the manner of a buffet, on a large serving table. It is not necessary to buy any special dishes or serving pieces. Attractive china of Western or Oriental design is appropriate. A well-arranged table setting will gladden the eye. It is desirable that the dinnerware be of various sizes and shapes. Most Chinese food should be served on platters, with the exception of rice and soup, which are, of course, served in bowls.

CHAPTER 5

Buying Hints

BUYING HINTS

IN THE *Analects* we are told that Confucius would not eat food that was stale or out of season. Freshness in food is almost an obsession with the Chinese. As connoisseurs they love the flavor of the trout just plucked from the stream, the chicken just snatched from the barnyard, vegetables still jeweled with the morning dew. There are subtle grace notes in food which are often lost after the first bloom. The Chinese cooks would travel for miles to bargain the market known for the purity and freshness of its produce, since they felt that buying was an essential part of the culinary arts—in fact, buying the food was the sole prerogative of the head cook.

Living as they did in small villages near the field, stream, and barnyard, the Chinese did not find it difficult to indulge their taste for uncompromising freshness. In fact, they had no choice; they could not afford to compromise since there was no refrigeration. The simplest way to keep a chicken was to keep him running until the eleventh hour. The fish would continue to make their turns in the little pond created for them until the guests arrived, and the vegetables went on with their slow growth.

In the absence of refrigeration the Chinese developed various ways of preserving foods which had reached their prime and were in excess of the family needs. Drying was the most used method, and it was a common sight to see various foods hanging on lines in the yards to dry. Drying also brings out the flavor of certain foods such as mushrooms. Eggs were encased in lime and clay mixed with wheat chaff, so that no air would enter, and were buried for forty days. If you have ever been served one-hundred year old eggs it has most likely been a case of Chinese poetic exaggeration. Salting, smoking, and pickling were other methods which were frequently used.

The actual variety of Chinese foods exceeds anything known in the West. The gourmet, the traveler and the moderately well-to-do citizens of such cosmopolitan cities as Peking and Shanghai had an almost unlimited selection of delectables. For most people, however, the actual choice of foods was not so splendid and was in many areas severely limited by difficulties in transportation as well as by economic factors. Many delectable Chinese foods are available only in a certain area at certain times of the year. Winter in a lonely rural outpost offered a dreary selection of foods to the average family and was a challenge to the culinary skills of the Chinese wife.

There was something about the Chinese bazaar with its swarms of flies and continuous parley that brought out the sharp trader in everyone. Those fellows had to be watched. It was an old market trick to fill the customers baskets with wilted produce which bore no relationship to the gorgeous foods on display.

The American market, in contrast, offers conveniences and amenities which were unknown in the open markets. There is a nice absence of chicanery, but one must still look sharp in the produce department.

We have found that the major mistakes in buying are made in selection of fruits and vegetables. The error which most of us tend to make is to buy too great a quantity at one time; it is a temptation to buy five heads of lettuce because they are on sale or a flat of peaches because they look so luscious. Try to visualize how everything will look in the refrigerator at the end of the week, then make your purchases accordingly. It is better to buy too little than too much, even if it means a brief visit to the market toward the end of the week. It is difficult to say which is worse: the waste of throwing out vegetables, or the thought of cooking them after their prime.

The second mistake which is often made in buying produce is the meek acceptance of inferior quality. Many housewives will buy rusty lettuce, limp celery and other abominations simply because it is there. Many supermarkets bring in their big loads of produce on Thursday for the weekend shopping, then sell the excess to customers on Monday, Tuesday, and Wednesday. It is a good idea to find when the fresh shipments arrive at your neighborhood store and arrange to be there. If you find your store trying to unload tired specimens, "ring the little bell," and ask for the fresh produce in the back. Usually a beautiful selection will appear on demand. If the situation does not improve, ask for the manager; he is usually sensitive to comments of this kind. It is important to remember that vegetables must be of good quality for Chinese cooking.

The third mistake in buying vegetables is picking out the largest on the theory that the biggest means the best. In vegetables the converse is often true, and the Chinese always look for the smallest ones. *Young* and *tender* are the adjectives which, to the Chinese, mean quality in vegetables. The flavor and texture of young vegetables is better than their overgrown brothers, and the extra work required in washing, paring, and cutting small vegetables is well worth it. Large vegetables are not only tough, they often tend to be flavorless. Growers in certain parts of the country are turning out large and gorgeous fruits and vegetables because so many customers are impressed with size. They also tend to be watery and without flavor.

Now that American supermarkets are beginning to stock Chinese foods, it is not always necessary for Americans to make a trip to Chinatown to find such things as celery cabbage and snow peas. Often these Chinese foods are as fresh and as reasonably priced in the American market as they are in the Chinese market. On the other hand, great savings can be made in buying such staples as rice and noodles in the Chinese market. The price of these foods is very dependent on the quantity sold and the manner of packaging. The cost of handling and packaging small amounts of rice and noodles is inversely proportionate to the quantity. The Chinese markets sell rice five pounds at a time, inexpensively packaged, at a price which is a real bargain to the housewife. Thus we give our American students this strange advice: buy Chinese foods at the American market whenever you can, and American food at the Chinese market if you wish to save money.

The growth of the large food chains has eliminated the man in the middle and has resulted in a lowering of the cost of many foods. Some foods are priced close to the wholesale level, and many of the "loss leaders" are actually priced below wholesale. Most American housewives hunt for these "specials," and we heartily endorse this practice. These foods are usually of high quality. We must, however, warn against a new custom which is unfortunately being used to deceive the customer in certain stores. Foods are marked "on sale" although the price has not been lowered.

Another practice which we recommend is the buying of the "house brands" of the large national supermarkets. These are the foods which are packaged by the food chains themselves; they usually compare favorably with the nationally advertised brands, and they are usually considerably lower in price.

In this age of the impersonal supermarket, we feel that it is still important for the housewife to know the people she is dealing with. The butcher and the manager of the supermarket can be valuable friends. They are usually glad to meet a customer who is giving them most of her food dollar, they are good sources of information, and they will often give their strong customers special privileges. They will tell you, for example, when the supplies of fresh produce are coming in, when certain foods are going on sale, and facts about the quality of two competitive items. One piece of information which is worth having is the day on which the fresh fish arrives. It is usually Thursday or Friday, in most localities. In some supermarkets, fish is sold which is not absolutely fresh.*

The store manager will often give a good customer a special price if she buys food in quantity. One of our friends buys ground steak at the price of hamburger because she has timed her arrival at the meat counter twenty minutes before closing time on Saturday. There is usually a large supply of ground steak left over, but the

---

* Certain fish and sea foods are not available in supermarkets and may only be found in large fish markets.

hamburger is usually gone. She will ask the butcher for hamburger. He will wink slyly, remove the ground steak from the counter and relabel it hamburger. Whenever there is a sale on items which keep well, she will ask for a case price. Sometimes she will receive a discount, sometimes the manager will explain that he is already losing money on that item.

Even though the supermarket treats its customers like robots, it is not necessary to act like one. It is important to remember that there is a great competition for your food dollar, and the total food purchases of the average American family represent a great deal of bargaining power.

Chinese cooking requires a great variety of ingredients and condiments. One should therefore, keep a fairly constant supply of staples and condiments on the kitchen shelves and have a reserve shelf for emergencies. The following ingredients should be held in readiness at all times:

rice: buy from Chinese market
noodles: buy from Chinese market
dried garlic, garlic powder: in case you run short of garlic
dried onions: in case you find yourself without scallions
dry sherry
soy sauce
peanut or sesame oil
pepper
ginger: fresh, dried, or powdered
canned bamboo shoots
canned bean sprouts
canned chicken stock
canned water chestnuts
canned or frozen shrimp
canned or frozen crabmeat
tinned whole hams
canned mushrooms
dried mushrooms

The following ingredients must be replenished frequently, and it is important to judge the proper quantity to buy. If you buy too much you will find that foods are eaten past their prime or thrown out. If you buy too little, you may find yourself wondering what you will eat. Mrs. Lee's students plan a week's menus ahead of time. They will save parts of a roast pork for the next evening's meal, and always have the "makings" of quick meals and snacks in the refrigerator or freezer.

Vegetables

Count on buying these:
- bean sprouts
- celery
- celery cabbage
- cabbage
- mushrooms
- scallions
- fresh ginger (if available)

Buy in season:
- asparagus
- cucumbers
- snow peas
- summer squash

Also of interest:
- green peppers
- spinach
- zuccini

Meat

Pork is the choice meat for Chinese cooking

Chicken and duck—you may keep one or two frozen for reserve

Ham: Frequently used in Chinese cooking, seldom eaten in large quantities. Save left-over ham for Chinese cooking; small families might require one or more slices of ham.

Many of our recipes call for small amounts of meat and sea food. We do not expect our students to go to the market and ask for one-fourth pound of chicken, or a few shrimp. There is a knack of managing food in the refrigerator in order to cook in the Chinese style. Chinese cooking requires small amounts of a wide variety of foods; the American housewife is used to dealing with fairly large amounts of a limited number of ingredients. Habits must, therefore, be adjusted somewhat in order to cope with a new style of cooking. Certain foods must be kept on hand at all times in order to avoid a last-minute shortage of some critical ingredient. Menus should be planned in advance, so that the chicken, ham, mushrooms, or bean sprouts can be used in more than one dish.

One buys a small boneless ham and whittles away at it for a week or so. Bits of ham make their appearance in fried rice with ham and eggs, chao mein, chicken and ham soup. A whole chicken is bought. The breast and thighs go into chao dishes and the rest goes into the stewing pot. Some cooks prefer to buy the chicken by the part and keep a package of chicken breasts in the tray under the freezer. They will keep better and be easier to slice paper thin if they are kept in a semifrozen state. Shrimp with their shells on may be bought by the pound and stored in the freezer for two weeks; they may then be drawn off as needed for a shrimp omelet, or sub gum chao mein.

A Note on Mushrooms

The Chinese prefer dried mushrooms in most of their dishes. In China drying was the usual way to deal with mushrooms in the absence of hothouses and refrigerators. While the taste of dried mushrooms may be strong for the American palate, they are heartily recommended over canned or fresh ones in the savory stew recipes, as their flavor harmonizes with these robust dishes. The only dish in which dried mushrooms must not be used is Marinated Mushrooms. This recipe *must* be made with fresh mushrooms. In most recipes, canned mushrooms may be substituted for fresh.

Dried mushrooms are washed in cool water, then soaked in warm water for a minimum of 15 minutes, to develop the flavor, before use. An hour is preferable if time allows.

A Note on Cabbage

The heart of cabbage is the center of garden-variety American cabbage—the part that is often thrown away in American households. The Chinese believe that the heart is the best part of a vegetable.

When "cabbage" is called for, we mean plain American cabbage. "Celery cabbage" is also known as napa or Chinese cabbage. It is shaped somewhat like romaine. It is white at the root end and green at the crinkly tips. It has a clear flavor somewhere between cabbage and lettuce.

In areas where celery cabbage cannot be obtained, American cabbage can be substituted. In recipes calling for both cabbage and celery cabbage, the quantity of plain cabbage can be increased if celery cabbage is not available.

Bok choy may be difficult to find in some markets. It looks like green celery and tastes a little like broccoli with with a light taste of Brussels sprouts. If the market carries it there will be a sign, "bok choy."

Water chestnuts and bamboo shoots are very expensive for family meals. Each item runs from thirty-seven to forty-one cents a can. For economy reasons they may be omitted and heart of celery or cabbage, celery, or some other vegetable substituted.

After a while our students become very adept at planning Chinese dishes, and they begin to think of their refrigerators as banks full of little treasures.

CHAPTER 6

Into the Chinese Kitchen

THE CHINESE KITCHEN

THE kitchen was the kingdom of the chef—the lord of the pots and pans. It was necessary for the cook in a large household to be a good organizer, since there were so many courses to prepare daily and so many dishes which required split-second timing. A Chinese banquet is a play in which each dish must make an entrance at the proper moment.

In a wealthy household there would be several apprentice cooks under the master chef. It was a strange apprenticeship, since the head cook did not really want to teach his underlings anything. Why should he tell them all his secrets? Nonetheless, he usually did, for he wished to preserve his importance by assigning everything to his assistants. He would trade his knowledge for long naps in the afternoon. As he delegated more and more of the work to his assistants, he was unwillingly forming another generation of Chinese cooks. Thus in its own peculiar fashion the Chinese culinary art was passed down through the centuries.

The actual cooking was not so whimsical, however. The Chinese kitchen was more than a kitchen—it was a laboratory, a factory, a marvel of efficiency. Over the centuries the Chinese culinary arts have became so scientific that the preparation of a dish resembles an experiment in a laboratory by a team of research scientists.

The Chinese cook uses a minimum of equipment. Give him a *wok* (pan), a pair of chop sticks, and a good sharp knife and he can turn out any dish in short order. There is a certain advantage in simplicity: the fewer implements, the fewer things to be bothered with.

We feel, however, that the American housewife should use the equipment which she has found to be satisfactory in her everyday cooking. She will probably find that her pancake turner makes a very good stirring instruments for *chao* dishes, and that she can wield it more easily than a set of chop sticks. However, a wooden spoon is preferable since it does not bruise the ingredients.

Some of our students use *woks* or *kuos* (Chinese frying pan), and some do not. It is a matter of personal choice. The *wok* holds the heat well, and its spherical shape is ideal for quick and constant stirring. On the other hand, it can be awkward to use if you have an electric stove. Since it has a rounded bottom, it must rest on an iron ring if the burner does not have a depression. Like the old fashioned cast-iron skillet, it is black and rather sooty and may not appeal to the fastidious soul who prefers gleaming pots and pans.

Our students tend to use the utensils in their own cupboards and have cooked Chinese foods successfully with all kinds of pots and pans. On the whole, however, heavy pans seem to work out better than light ones. The cast iron skillet and the heavy aluminum frying pan hold the heat evenly and well. The electric frying pan is a favorite of many of our students since it is deep and heavy and has a precise temperature control.

We have written our recipes with the average American kitchen in mind. No special equipment is required.

SOME HINTS FOR STORING FOODS

Vegetable bins and hydrators should be washed out with a mild disinfectant once a week to retard spoilage.

Rice, noodles, and dry vegetables should be kept in cool, dark places away from the heat, light, and moisture, which are the enemies of vitamins.

Meat should be wrapped in order to minimize the contact with air. Transparent plastic wrapping is good for this purpose.

Perishable vegetables should not be exposed to room temperatures any longer than necessary. Cold temperatures preserve the vitamin content. These vegetables should be kept in a covered hydrator, preferably on a rack over an eighth inch of water to supply continuous moisture.

PREPARATION FOR COOKING

"A minimum of cooking and a maximum of preparation" should be a motto for everyone who sets out to cook in the Chinese manner. Much of the actual cooking goes very rapidly and requires split-second timing; this is no time to wonder where you put the soy sauce. Everything must be in readiness for this culinary moment of truth, or the dish will not come off. The decks should be cleared and washed, all debris disposed of, no dishes in the sink, plates arranged for serving—*then* proceed. We have found that there is nothing more demoralizing and time wasting than to work in a disorderly kitchen. It may seem to take more time to clean as you go, but it really saves time in the long run. Moreover, food flavors transfer usually in an undesirable way. If you have cut onion on a board, it should be washed well before using it to cut celery or anything else. Some of our students save one side of their cutting board just for onions, or have a special cutting board just for this purpose. It is, of course, necessary to wash the hands thoroughly before cooking; many cooks, however, do not know that they should also wash their hands during the cooking after handling certain ingredients so that the flavors of food are not mingled in the preparation.

WASHING FOODS

Meat

Most meat in the United States does not require washing. The cavities of fowl should be rinsed in cold water before they are cooked.

Fish and Sea Food

Rinse in salted water.

Vegetables

See chapter on vegetables.

Dried and Salted Foods

Dried mushrooms and other dried foods are washed in cold water. The water is changed, and they are allowed to soak in warm water to develop the taste. Fresh mushrooms must be washed thoroughly in warm water.

Rice

Store without washing. Rinse under running water in fine colander until the water which runs off the rice is almost clear.

Noodles

Never wash. Water should be brought to a rolling boil before the noodles are added.

CUTTING, KNIVES AND TECHNIQUES

Cutting

Proper cutting has always been an essential part of the Chinese culinary arts. In the *Analects* we are told that Confucius would not eat if the food were not finely minced or the meat cut properly. Proper cutting accomplishes many things in Chinese cooking. It is especially important in the harmonic dishes where ingredients of different sizes and temperaments must be married. The proper cutting creates a harmonious appearance and permits the interpenetration of the flavors of the ingredients. Flavors are more easily exchanged between small pieces of food with cut facets than between large solid pieces. Finely cut foods require only a short period of cooking time. The flavors therefore are preserved and overcooking is avoided. Mushrooms, for example, may be cut in various ways in order to harmonize with their partners. With peas we would use button mushrooms and quarter their caps so that they were of approximately the same size as the peas. If the mushrooms were to

be served with noodles or bean sprouts, we would use larger mushrooms and cut them in long strips. The general rule is very simple:
cut everything in a uniform size.

Lastly, the cutting of food into bite sizes before it is served at the
table eliminates the use of the table knife, an instrument which the
Chinese used to consider barbaric, but which they now consider
an annoying distraction.

Proper cutting is based on an understanding of the textures of
foods. Carrots and asparagus, for example, are often cut on the
diagonal to expose more surface to the heat, permit them to cook
quickly to tenderness.

Knives

The Chinese cook works with a cleaverlike knife, a formidable
instrument which can dismember a fowl or do fine mincing. There
is nothing that can match it for efficiency. The blade is rectangular,
about three inches wide and nine inches long. The weight of the
blade does the work, and it is possible to cut smartly through foods
without the tedium of sawing back and forth.

Mrs. Lee works with a lady's version of this knife. It is less formidable, and our students find it very easy and safe to use. These knives
may be bought for a dollar and a half in Chinese markets. They
often have bamboo handles. Many of our students use a wide,
pointed French chef's knife. If you cannot find the Chinese knife,
use any wide, sharp knife with a straight blade.

Considering the amount of cutting which is necessary in Chinese
cooking, it is important to use a good knife and to keep it very sharp.
A dull knife bruises the food. A narrow-bladed or curved knife
means tedious cutting; it wastes time and strength, and does not
cut clean.

Cutting Boards

The traditional Chinese chopping block is a slab of wood at least
six inches thick. A good-sized chopping or cutting board is important in Chinese cooking.

Cutting Techniques

Straight cutting: Meat and certain vegetables such as celery cabbage are cut straight across the grain to protect succulence and tenderness.

Diagonal cutting: Carrots and asparagus are cut diagonally.

Mincing: Cut as fine as possible with a chopping motion. Although mincing meat is tedious, the flavor is so superior to ground meat that the Chinese feel that it is worth the trouble. If you use ground meat in Chinese recipes, have it ground only once on the coarse setting.

Dicing: Large mincing. Cut first in one direction and then crosshatch in the other, as in a grid-work.

Shredding: Thin slicing into pieces which are one inch square at the most. Cut as thin as possible.

Stripping: Cut into matchsticks, 1 to 1½ inches in length, as thin as possible.

Paring: The little dime-store gadget is fine for this purpose. Cucumbers and other vegetables are pared.

Trimming: Cut off the tough parts of vegetables, such as the ends of string beans. Meat should be trimmed of all fat before it is cooked.

Dismember fowl: The usual Chinese method is to cut the pieces into two-inch lengths with the bone left in, so that the pieces can be picked up with chopsticks. The author feels that cutting in large pieces has certain advantages, however; the larger pieces are easier to cut, and they retain the juices and flavor better than small ones. To cut poultry you may use a cleaver as the Chinese do, or you can use a poultry shears. Where thin slices of poultry or any other meat are required, it is helpful to freeze the meat partially. A very sharp knife is also obligatory.

Shrimp and sea food: Devein and cut to conform to the size and shapes of other ingredients in the dish.

Vegetables: Further detailed instructions will be given in the chapter on vegetables.

CHAPTER 7

Traditional Chinese Cooking Methods

EVERY Chinese dish has its own appropriate cooking method. There must be harmony between the nature of the ingredients and the amount of heat. Correct timing and right temperature are essential if the dish is to be right. Certain methods seal in the juices, others draw them out; some methods preserve the crispness of foods, others break down coarse or tough texture. The degree and duration of heat has a decisive effect on the flavor and texture of the dish. We will now describe the traditional cooking methods which are used in China.

1. CHIEN. The ingredients are sautéed in a small amount of oil over a gentle fire until one side is a golden brown. They are then turned, and the other side is browned. In the West, we use this method frequently to cook such foods as lamb chops, cube steaks, and filet of sole. Low heat preserves the flavor and tenderness of meats.

2. CHAO. A characteristic Chinese method of hot frying. The ingredients are fried in a little oil over a quick fire and must be stirred constantly until done—usually for only a few minutes.

3. PON. The ingredients are cooked over a quick, hot fire with the basic sauce which is made of soy sauce, sherry, sugar, salt, and MSG. The technique is identical with *Chao* (hot frying), except that the basic sauce is used instead of oil. The ingredients must be stirred constantly.

4. TSA. Deep frying. The oil must be very hot before introducing the ingredients. The ingredients must be dry, or the moisture will

cause splattering. Many foods, with the exception of those which require only a few minutes' cooking time such as shrimp, cannot be cooked properly if this method is used alone. Meat and poultry will either be raw on the inside, or burned on the outside, or both. In some cases, the food breaks in pieces. The meat of certain kinds of poultry, such as squab, duck, and pheasant, must be precooked by steaming or simmering with condiments until it is almost done. Then it is browned in the hot fat, and the result will be golden brown on the outside and tender and fully cooked on the inside. Deep frying to be successful must be done quickly. Fish should be coated with cornstarch to preserve its flavor and keep it intact. The amount of oil which is needed is not great. A depth of 2 inches is usually sufficient to deep fry most foods. The oil is always saved for future use, except when fish have been fried.

5. Ao. Simmering over a low fire with the pot covered to avoid evaporation. The lid should never be removed.

6. Shao. Stewing various condiments and ingredients together over a fairly high fire for a long time. This method is used to marry the juice of the meat with the vegetables, and to enhance the flavor of the dish with condiments. This method is divided into two kinds of cooking:

Red cooking with soy sauce for a red-brown gravy, a favorite method of home cooking for the Chinese. In China, red-cooked meats take the place of family roasts in the United States.

White cooking is stewing without soy sauce.

In both methods the ingredients may be treated by prefrying, but many cooks prefer to eliminate this step.

7. Men. Stewing on top of the stove in a deep, covered pan over a low fire.

8. Chu. Boiling. Seldom used alone, since the Chinese believe it destroys flavor and nutritional value. Noodles are cooked by this method. Some foods are precooked by parboiling, but only for a minute or two.

9. Cheng. Steaming on a rack over boiling water on a moderate fire. The Chinese use this method a great deal, since the juices,

flavors, and nutritional values of food are conserved. In the United States where few women have equipment for steaming, a double boiler may be substituted for *Cheng* recipes, though steaming is preferable. If you would like to make a steamer, simply take an aluminum pie tin and perforate it with many holes. On the bottom of a deep pan which has a tight-fitting lid, place an old cup, right side up. Place the inverted pie tin inside the pan, resting it on top of the cup. The tin should be about the same diameter as the pan. Place about 2 inches of water in the pan for steaming.

10. KAO. Barbecuing over charcoal on a spit or a grill, similar to a hibachi. Rotisseries can be used for cooking by this method.

11. DUN. Simmering in a covered pan for at least one hour with clear soup.

12. HUI. "Associating." Two or more precooked ingredients are introduced to each other with a moderate amount of liquid ingredients in order to marry the flavors. Cooked leftovers are often combined and cooked according to this principle.

13. LUN-BAN. Cold mixing. Combining cold ingredients, as in Chinese salads. In China, the greens were usually scalded or parboiled quickly, for hygienic reasons, then chilled.

14. CHIN-WAI. Marinating. Foods are soaked in various kinds of marinades for different lengths of time. Soy sauce and wine have a purifying effect on the odors and tastes of food. Fish is often marinated in soy sauce and wine to remove the fishiness; it is essential in baking and steaming fish. Liver is also treated in this manner. Steak and other meats, however, are often toughened by soy sauce, and, therefore, are soaked in pure sesame oil instead; this treatment makes the meat tender on the inside and crisp on the outside.

15. PAI. Pounding. Meat is pounded with a cleaver to make it tender and loose. Cut across the grain.

CHINESE COOKING IN THE AMERICAN HOUSEHOLD

Chinese cookery can be bewildering. Chinese recipes in their original state can be followed only by an experienced cook, since they are more of an inspiration than an instruction. To the Western mind, the recipes used by Chinese cooks are in a state of anarchy, since nothing was measured accurately—if measured at all. The catty, which was the Chinese unit of measurement, was never standardized, and it meant one thing in Canton and another in Shanghai. To the Chinese chef, however, the state of the culinary arts was serene, logical, and scientific. From a mere suggestion, he could compose any dish because he knew the fundamental cooking methods and the proper proportion of ingredients. It was not necessary for him to measure anything, since he had studied cooking for years under a master chef, and instinctively used the right amount of each ingredient.

In China, there are thousands of dishes, and each dish has many variations. After one has studied Chinese cookery for many years, however, one begins to see patterns and similarities, and is able to distinguish the proverbial forest from the trees. To emphasize the essential principles of the art, we have presented each recipe in the same manner in order to understand the structure of the various dishes. Every recipe is viewed as a variation of a basic principle. We have grouped similar recipes together as much as possible. Although many recipes are based on the same principle, we must remember that each dish is unique and has its own character and flavor because it differs in ingredients, timing, and proportion from the other recipes in its group.

In China, it is the basic principle which matters, not the recipe. Recipes are variations of basic principles; they are ideas of which foods will harmonize in an interesting fashion, and the timing and proportion are scientifically geared to the nature of the ingredients.

Pork, for example, requires more cooking time than beef; chicken and shrimp take up more cooking oil than pork. Certain vegetables require a preliminary parboiling; others do not.

The recipes have been reduced to their logical essence. Through the elimination of unnecessary steps and through the use of modern technological developments, the recipes in this book average no more than twenty minutes cooking time, with the exception of dishes which can be left on the stove to simmer without the cook's attention. We teach our students that it takes no more time to cook with distinction than to put together an ordinary meal.

All the recipes have been tested by American housewives in their homes and are, therefore, suited to the arrangement of the American household and the likes and dislikes of husbands and children. Although we follow orthodox Chinese principles of cookery, we have made revisions in some of the original methods whenever they have seemed unbearable in the context of American life; there will be no soaking of chicken legs on window sills, no preserving of eggs with lime and mud on bright formica countertops, no hanging of foods to dry in the window, no soaking of exotic sea creatures for three months on top of the refrigerator. The methods we describe are neat, hygienic, and aesthetic.

Before you begin to cook, the ingredients schould be completely cut and placed in small bowls or piled on a tray near the stove.

Often a group of condiments will be bracketed in the recipes to indicate that they should be combined in a sauce, a marinade, or a paste. Combine all bracketed items in small bowls. Cooking oil is listed on the right, since it is considered a condiment by the Chinese. Cornstarch, stock, and water are "floaters" and will sometimes appear in one column and sometimes in another, depending on the manner in which they are used in the recipe. If cornstarch is bracketed with water or stock, it should be made into a creamy paste a few seconds before it is required.

Adding Oil

The pan must always be heated thoroughly before the oil is added, and the oil heated thoroughly before the ingredients are added. Otherwise the dish will be sticky.

Temperatures

Where it is possible, we have given the approximate temperatures at which these dishes should be cooked, but in spite of our efforts we cannot achieve the precision we would like. The heaviness and shape of the pan has a great influence on the proper temperature. *Woks* (Chinese pans) require more heat than stainless steel frying pans. A cook who stirs constantly can cook with a much higher heat than one who does so sporadically.

Cornstarch

Cornstarch can be mixed thoroughly with water or cold stock. Do not leave the cornstarch in the solution for any length of time or it will become lumpy. It must be constantly stirred during cooking, and it should be cooked quickly and evenly, or the sauce will not have the smoothness which is a quality by which Chinese gourmets judge good food.

To facilitate the standardization of the recipes, we have made the number of people which each recipe will serve constant throughout the book. *Each recipe serves from four to six.* You may halve the recipe for two to three people, or double it for ten to twelve. The number of people which each recipe will serve depends, of course, on the number of dishes which are to be served at the meal and the state of each diner's appetite.

CHAPTER 8

Hors d'Oeuvres and Canapes

In China, hors d'oeuvres are called *dien-hsing*—"strike-the-heart." There are thousands of varieties of these little delights and everyone is very fond of them. In cities such as Peking and Canton, there were restaurants which served nothing but hors d'oeuvres with tea or wine. These places were the Chinese equivalent of the coffee houses and bars which are so much a part of the student life of Paris and New York.

These golden brown canapes and hors d'oeuvres are best when served hot from the fire, but they may be kept warm in a 200° oven.

SHRIMP, CRAB OR LOBSTER TOAST

Serves 4 to 6   Method: Deep frying

Ingredients

1 lb fresh shrimp, crab or lobster, cleaned and minced
1 Tbs cornstarch
1 dry onion, finely diced
2 eggs
8 slices of trimmed bread, each cut into 4 triangular pieces
1 cup bamboo shoots, diced (optional)

Condiments

Mix Sauce
{
2 Tbs soy sauce
1 Tbs sherry
1 tsp salt
⅛ tsp MSG
1 thin slice ginger, minced, or dash of ginger powder
}

peanut oil for deep frying

74

METHOD

1. Mix shrimp (or crab or lobster), cornstarch, onion, 1 well-beaten egg, and sauce. (Add bamboo shoots if used.)
2. Spoon mixture ¾-inch thick on the bread triangles. Smooth into a gentle dome.
3. Brush all the hors d'oeuvres with the second beaten egg to glaze.
4. Heat 2 inches of peanut oil in the frying pan to 350°.
5. Deep fry the bread triangles to a golden brown.
6. Drain on paper towels.

SHRIMP OR CRAB BALLS WITH WATER CHESTNUTS

SERVES 4 to 6   METHOD: Deep frying

INGREDIENTS

1 lb fresh shrimp or crab, cleaned and minced

1 cup canned water chestnuts, diced

CONDIMENTS

Mix Sauce
- 2 Tbs soy sauce
- 1 Tbs sherry
- 1 tsp salt
- 1 tsp sugar
- 1 clove garlic, crushed
- 1 thin slice ginger, diced
- ⅛ tsp MSG
- 3 Tbs cornstarch
- 3 eggs, beaten

peanut oil for deep frying

METHOD

1. Mix the shrimp or crabmeat and water chestnuts with the sauce.
2. Heat 2 inches of peanut oil in the frying pan to 350°.
3. Spoon the mixture into the hot fat, a tablespoon at a time. Fry until golden brown.
4. Serve hot or put in a 200° oven until ready to serve.

CHINESE MEATBALLS

SERVES 4 to 6   METHOD: Deep frying

INGREDIENTS   CONDIMENTS

1 lb ground lean pork
¼ cup mushrooms, finely chopped
1 cup water chestnuts, minced
2 Tbs cornstarch
1 egg

Mix Sauce:
⎧ 2 Tbs soy sauce
⎪ 1 Tbs sherry
⎪ ¼ tsp salt
⎨ ⅛ tsp MSG
⎪ 1 tsp sugar
⎪ 1 clove garlic, crushed
⎩ 1 small ginger slice, minced,
    or a pinch of ginger powder

peanut oil for deep frying

METHOD

1. Mix all ingredients with the exception of cornstarch. Add the sauce.
2. Sprinkle meat mixture with cornstarch.
3. Roll balls, 1 inch in diameter.
4. Deep fry at 350° in a hot pan until golden brown, approximately 8-10
   minutes. Serve hot.

FRIED BUTTERFLY SHRIMP

SERVES 4 to 6   METHOD: Deep frying

INGREDIENTS   CONDIMENTS

1 lb fresh shrimp, shelled,
  and deveined
2 eggs, beaten
1½ Tbs cornstarch
1½ Tbs flour

Mix Batter

Marinade:
⎧ 1 Tbs soy sauce
⎪ 1 tsp sherry
⎨ ½ tsp salt
⎪ ⅛ tsp MSG
⎩ 1 slice ginger, diced

peanut oil for deep frying

METHOD

1. Cut shrimp halfway through on inner curve, and spread out to form butterfly.
2. Marinate shrimp in sauce for at least 15 minutes. Remove and dry thoroughly.
3. Dip the shrimp into the batter and coat well.
4. Heat 2 inches of peanut oil to 350° in a frying pan.
5. Fry the shrimp until golden brown. Serve hot.

SKEWERED HORS D'OEUVRES

These miniature kebobs are very tasty party fare. They may be threaded on toothpicks, small skewers, or on small bamboo sticks in the Chinese fashion. They may be deep fried, broiled, or cooked by the guests on a *hibachi*.

They may be prepared the day before the party and popped onto the fire when the guests arrive. Although they are best when they are eaten immediately after they are cooked, they may be reheated in a 200° oven for late guests.

GOLDEN DOLLARS

SERVES 4 to 6   METHOD: Deep frying

INGREDIENTS   CONDIMENTS

1 lb shredded cooked chicken breasts, cut in 1-inch rounds like golden dollars

¼ lb sliced precooked ham, cut in same size as chicken

6 water chestnuts, sliced (three slices from every chestnut) (optional)

2 Tbs cornstarch ⎫
3 Tbs water   ⎬ Mix Batter
2 eggs   ⎭

Marinade ⎧ 2 Tbs soy sauce
         ⎪ 1 Tbs sherry
         ⎪ 1 Tbs brown sugar
         ⎨ 1 scallion, diced
         ⎪ ⅛ tsp MSG
         ⎪ 1 small slice ginger, diced,
         ⎩   or a pinch of ginger powder

peanut oil for deep frying

METHOD

1. Marinate chicken breasts in sauce for half an hour or more.
2. Thread rounds of chicken, ham, and chestnut on a skewer and dip in egg batter.
3. Deep fry in oil at 350° until golden brown, or broil in oven or on a hibachi.
4. Serve hot, or put in a 200° oven until ready to serve.

SKEWERED CHICKEN LIVERS

SERVES 4 to 6   METHOD: Deep frying or broiling

INGREDIENTS   CONDIMENTS

1 lb chicken livers, whole

Marinade
- 3 Tbs soy sauce
- 1 Tbs sherry
- 1 Tbs brown sugar
- 1 tsp salt
- ⅛ tsp MSG
- 1 small slice ginger, diced, or a dash of ginger powder
- 1 clove garlic crushed

peanut oil for deep frying

METHOD

1. Parboil chicken livers in salted water for 2 minutes.
2. Marinate the chicken livers for ½ to 3 hours.
3. Thread chicken livers on skewers.
4. Deep fry in oil at 375° until golden brown, or broil in oven or on a hibachi.

SKEWERED CHICKEN WITH BACON

SERVES 4 to 6   METHOD: Deep frying or broiling

INGREDIENTS   **CONDIMENTS**

½ lb chicken, sliced
   paper thin
½ lb bacon, cut in 1-inch pieces
5 water chestnuts, sliced
   paper thin

Marinade
- 3 Tbs soy sauce
- 1 Tbs sherry
- 1 Tbs brown sugar
- 1 tsp salt
- ⅛ tsp MSG
- 1 small slice ginger, diced,
  or a dash of ginger powder
- 1 clove garlic crushed

Glaze
- 2 Tbs soy sauce
- 2 Tbs honey

peanut oil for deep frying

METHOD

1. Marinate the chicken for ½ to 3 hours.
2. Thread chicken, water chestnuts, and bacon on skewers. Brush with glaze.
3. Deep fry in oil at 375° until golden brown, or broil in an oven or on a hibachi.

SKEWERED CHICKEN WITH HAM

SERVES 4 to 6   METHOD: Deep frying or broiling

INGREDIENTS   **CONDIMENTS**

½ lb chicken, sliced
   paper thin
½ lb cooked sliced ham, cut in
   1-inch pieces

Marinade
- 3 Tbs soy sauce
- 1 Tbs sherry
- 1 Tbs brown sugar
- 1 tsp MSG
- 1 small slice ginger, diced,
  or a dash of ginger powder
- 1 clove garlic crushed

$$\text{Glaze} \begin{cases} \text{2 Tbs soy sauce} \\ \text{2 Tbs honey} \end{cases}$$

peanut oil for deep frying

METHOD

1. Marinate the chicken for ½ to 3 hours.
2. Thread chicken, and ham on skewers. Glaze with mixture.
3. Deep fry in oil at 375° until golden brown brown, or broil in an oven or on a hibachi.

SPARERIBS

The secret of cooking spareribs properly is to cook them thoroughly and evenly; the excess oil must be allowed to drip off during the cooking process, since spareribs are a fat meat.

Spareribs must always be marinated for a few hours or overnight so that the flavor of the sauce penetrates the meat. If they are left in the marinade for more than 12 hours, however, they will become tough.

Spareribs should be baked in a moderate oven because long cooking at a high heat tends to shrivel them. For crispness, the oven should be very hot for the last five minutes of cooking. Broiling is usually unsatisfactory unless the spareribs are precooked; spareribs require long, even cooking, and broiled spareribs are usually burned or half-cooked or both.

In China, restaurants often hang spareribs from racks in large outdoor ovens. This permits the spareribs to cook evenly in dry heat. If the spareribs are cooked horizontally, part of the meat will steam. The hanging of the meat permits the excess grease to drip out during the cooking. You can achieve the same object in any American oven by running small, 3-inch skewers through the ribs 3 inches from the end and hanging them from the rack in your oven.

HANGING BARBECUED SPARERIBS

SERVES 4 to 6   METHOD: Barbecuing

INGREDIENTS   **CONDIMENTS**

2 lb spareribs

Marinade
- 1 cup soy sauce
- ½ cup catsup
- 2 Tbs sherry
- 2 Tbs brown sugar
- 1 tsp salt
- 2 cloves garlic, crushed
- 2 slices ginger, diced

Glaze
- 2 Tbs honey
- 1 tsp soy sauce

METHOD

1. Marinate spareribs for at least 2 hours. They may be left overnight in the marinade.
2. Skewer the spareribs 2 inches from the end. Hang from oven rack. Put a pan under the ribs to catch the dripping.
3. Bake in 325° oven for 1½ hours.
4. Brush with honey glaze. Raise heat to 450° to crisp the spareribs. Cook at this high heat for *no longer* than 5 minutes.
5. Serve hot. Or if necessary, keep in 200° oven until ready to serve. (If any spareribs are left over, you may reheat them the next day in a 350° oven.)

BARBECUED SPARERIBS

SERVES 4 to 6   METHOD: Barbecuing

INGREDIENTS   **CONDIMENTS**

2 lb spareribs, cut in 2-inch lengths
water to cover

Marinade
- 1 cup soy sauce
- ½ cup catsup
- 2 Tbs sherry
- 2 Tbs brown sugar
- 2 cloves garlic, crushed
- 2 slices ginger, diced

$$\text{Glaze} \begin{cases} \text{2 Tbs honey} \\ \text{1 tsp soy sauce} \end{cases}$$

$$\begin{matrix} \text{in cooking} \\ \text{water} \end{matrix} \begin{cases} \text{2 medium onions, diced} \\ \text{1 Tbs salt} \end{cases}$$

METHOD

1. Simmer spareribs with onions and salt for 1½ hours in covered pan. The water should almost cover the ribs—too much water ruins them. Remove and drain.
2. Marinate for 2 to 12 hours.
3. Bake on rack in 350° oven for 30 to 35 minutes.
4. Glaze with honey mixture. Raise heat to 450° and cook for *no longer* than 5 minutes.
5. Serve hot. Or if necessary, keep in a oven 200° until ready to serve. (If any spareribs are left, they may be warmed in a 350° oven the next day.) Spareribs may be prepared in advance and kept in freezer.

COLD PORK WITH HOT MUSTARD

SERVES 4 to 6   METHOD: Roasting

INGREDIENTS   **CONDIMENTS**

2 lb boneless pork roast

$$\begin{matrix} \text{Mix} \\ \text{Sauce} \end{matrix} \begin{cases} \text{1 cup soy sauce} \\ \text{½ cup sherry} \\ \text{½ cup brown sugar} \\ \text{1 tsp salt} \\ \text{⅛ tsp pepper} \\ \text{⅛ tsp MSG} \\ \text{1 medium dry onion, diced,} \end{cases}$$

$$\begin{matrix} \text{Hot} \\ \text{Mustard} \end{matrix} \begin{cases} \text{Mix dry mustard powder} \\ \text{with water to form a} \\ \text{creamy paste.} \end{cases}$$

METHOD

1. Put pork roast in roasting pan. Cover with sauce. Marinate for 2 hours.
2. Roast pork with sauce in 400° oven for 10 minutes.
3. Lower heat to 325° and continue to roast for 1 hour and 40 minutes or until done.
4. Put roast in the refrigerator and be sure that it is very cold before you slice it.
5. Slice in pieces as thin as a quarter and about 2½ inches long and 1 inch wide.
6. Arrange on a platter with mustard dip.

NOTE: Line the drip pan with aluminum foil, or it will be very hard to clean.

GOLDEN HOOKS

SERVES 4 to 6   METHOD: Baking

INGREDIENTS

1 lb unshelled shrimp
  (open back and devein)

CONDIMENTS

Mix Sauce
{
1 Tbs soy sauce
2 Tbs Worchestershire sauce
1 Tbs sherry
1 Tbs brown sugar
}

METHOD

1. Marinate shrimp in sauce for 30 minutes.
2. Put shrimp and sauce in a baking pan and bake at 300° for 25 minutes.
3. Serve hot or cold, in the shell. The guests shell their own.

BAKED HAM TURNOVERS

SERVES 4 to 6   METHOD: Baking

INGREDIENTS

PASTRY

3 cups all-purpose flour
1½ cup chicken fat, butter, or lard
½ cup water

Sesame seeds

FILLING

½ lb precooked ham, minced
1 cup bamboo shoots, minced
1 scallion, minced
1 Tbs soy sauce

METHOD

1. Make dough of fat, flour, and water.
2. Mix ham, bamboo shoots, scallion, and soy sauce.
3. For each turnover, use enough dough to make thin pancake about 2 inches in diameter; put meat ingredients in center; press ends together, sealing with water. After brushing turnover with water, sprinkle with sesame seeds.
4. Bake at 350° until golden brown, about 30 minutes.

DUMPLINGS I

SERVES 4 to 6   METHOD: Boiling

INGREDIENTS

PASTRY

4 cups flour
2 cups cold water

FILLING

1 lb cooked lean pork, beef, or chicken, minced
½ lb cooked shrimp, cleaned and diced
1 lb celery, spinach, or cabbage heart, diced (dry thoroughly)

Mix Sauce

1 Tbs soy sauce
1 Tbs sherry
1 Tbs sesame oil
1 tsp salt
⅛ tsp MSG
⅛ tsp pepper
1 scallion or 1 dry onion, finely minced
2 cloves garlic, crushed
1 slice ginger, thinly diced

METHOD

1. Mix the flour with the water to form a soft dough. Knead well.
2. Leave covered for 10 minutes.
3. Stretch and roll out the dough as thin as possible.
4. With a biscuit cutter, cut out circles 2 inches in diameter.
5. Mix the meat, shrimp, and vegetables with the sauce.
6. Place 1 tsp of the mixture in the center of each circle.
7. Fold over to make a semicircle. Press the edges with fingers, sealing them with water.
8. Bring water to boil in a deep pan. Gently lower the dumplings into the water.
9. When the dumplings rise to the top, add ¾ cup of cold water. The dumplings will sink for the second time. Bring the water to a boil.
10. When the dumplings rise again, they are done.

DUMPLINGS II

SERVES 4 to 6   METHOD: Deep frying

Make the dumplings according to the previous recipe. Save some or all of the dumplings and leave in the refrigerator overnight. When they are ready to be served, deep fry in hot fat at 350° until they are golden brown.

MARINATED MUSHROOMS

SERVES 4 to 6   METHOD: Marinating

INGREDIENTS

½ lb fresh, whole mushrooms

CONDIMENTS

Mix
Marinade
Sauce
{
2 Tbs soy sauce
1 Tbs sherry
⅛ tsp salt
1 Tbs sesame oil
1 drop Tabasco sauce
}

METHOD

1. Wash mushrooms thoroughly in cold water.
2. Put in colander. Slowly pour boiling water over mushrooms. Allow the mushrooms to dry thoroughly.
3. Pour marinade sauce over mushrooms. Marinate for 10 to 15 minutes.
4. Serve cold.

STUFFED MUSHROOMS

SERVES 4 to 6   METHOD: Steaming or simmering

INGREDIENTS   CONDIMENTS

½ lb crabmeat
    or
¼ lb uncooked shrimp, minced,
  and ¼ lb ground lean pork
5 water chestnuts, minced
1 egg white
1 Tbs cornstarch
24 large dried mushroom caps

Mix Sauce
{
1 Tbs soy sauce
1 Tbs sherry
⅛ tsp MSG
1 scallion, minced
}

METHOD

1. Clean mushrooms in cold water. Remove stems.
2. Soak in warm water for a few hours, or overnight. Squeeze dry before using.
3. Mix crabmeat and egg white thoroughly. Sprinkle with cornstarch. Add sauce.
4. Fill mushroom caps with crabmeat mixture.
5. Steam for 40 minutes. (You may make a steamer by adding a perforated rack to your dutch oven. This dish may also be simmered in a little water in a covered frying pan.)

SPRING ROLLS (EGG ROLLS)

SERVES 4 to 6

During the Chinese New Year, the entire country would take a month's vacation. For rich and poor alike it was a time to rest from the year's labors, a time of love, leisure, and the cultivation of the social arts. All activity ceased, the shops closed their doors, the servants and apprentices went back to their families.

The Chinese family would lay in provisions for a month and prepare to greet the many friends and relatives who would come to call. Guests were served tea and small rolls, the traditional food of the Chinese New Year. In the United States these rolls are known as "egg rolls," but the Chinese call them "Spring Rolls" because the Chinese New Year was followed by the first day of Spring.

PASTRY

The skins for spring rolls may be bought very reasonably in the Chinese market. They can however be made at home by the following method:

3 cups all purpose flour   Enough cold water to make a soft dough

METHOD

1. Add cold water to flour gradually and mix to form a soft dough.
2. Place dough on a well-floured board and cover for 10 minutes with a wet cloth.
3. Roll dough into a very thin sheet and cut into 2½ inch squares.

FILLING

INGREDIENTS

¼ lb uncooked chicken cut in strips

½ cup dried mushrooms, washed, soaked and cut in strips

2½ cups bean sprouts

½ cup bamboo shoots cut in strips

2 cups spinach cut in 1″ lengths

1 scallion, chopped finely

CONDIMENTS

Mix Sauce
{
2 Tbs soy sauce
1 Tbs sherry
½ tsp salt
⅛ tsp MSG
⅛ tsp pepper
}

2 Tbs peanut oil for frying

METHOD

1. Heat frying pan. Add oil and heat thoroughly.
2. Fry onion to a light golden.
3. Add chicken and quick fry for 4 minutes.
4. Add sauce and the rest of the ingredients and mix thoroughly. Quick fry for 2 minutes.
5. Put 1 Tbs of filling in the middle of each pastry square and roll into the shape of a sausage. Fold in ends, sealing with water.
6. Add 2 inches of peanut oil to a pan for deep frying. Heat to 360°.
7. Fry rolls to a golden brown. Lift out and drain on absorbent paper. Serve hot. These rolls may be reheated in the oven.

CHAPTER 9

Classic Chinese Food

HUNG-SHAO
(*Rich Savory Stewing*)

THE following recipes are *Hung-Shao* or red-cooked dishes. They are rich and savory stews which owe their reddish-brown color to soy sauce. In China, these dishes are the equivalent of roast beef, ham, and chicken. Fuel is scarce, and there are few families who have ovens for roasting. Stewing is the usual method used for family cooking. The *Shao* method is used; it means stewing. Anyone who has made beef stew knows how to cook these dishes.

It takes a certain amount of diligence to ruin these dishes. Time is relatively unimportant—they may simmer on the stove for one hour or several hours. They may be made a day ahead of time and may be served hot or cold. These dishes are wonderful to have in the refrigerator. They will keep beautifully for a week and may be reheated several times without harm.

Vegetables may be added to these dishes as a variation, but they should be added just before the dish is served and only to that quantity of the stew which will be eaten at one meal. Vegetables in a dish of this sort will not make good leftovers.

To serve the dish cold, pour it into a square mold and chill. The sauce will make a rich aspic. Only the plain meat dishes without vegetables should be served *en gelée*.

There are hundreds of *Hung-Shao* dishes in China. Shanghai especially is known for its *Hung-Shao* dishes. Although cooking procedures vary somewhat from dish to dish and province to province, the basic cooking method is the same for all *Hung-Shao* cooking. The authors have studied the various kinds of rich savory stews and have reduced the cooking procedure to its logical essence. Nonetheless, each dish remains unique because of differences in ingredients, timing, and proportion.

SAVORY CHICKEN

SERVES 4 to 6

METHOD: Stewing

INGREDIENTS

2½ to 3 lb chicken, cut into
  6 or 8 pieces
1½ cups water

1 Tbs cornstarch ⎱ Mix
2 Tbs water   ⎰ Thickening

CONDIMENTS

Mix Sauce ⎱ ½ cup soy sauce
     2 Tbs dry sherry
     2 Tbs brown sugar
     1 tsp salt

2 Tbs peanut oil for frying
3 scallions or ½ medium
  dry onion, stripped
2 cloves garlic, crushed
2 thin slices ginger

METHOD

1. Heat deep skillet (350°). Add oil. Quick fry chicken until golden brown.

2. Drain excess oil. Add scallions, garlic, and ginger, and quick fry with chicken for 2 minutes.

3. Add sauce and mix well with chicken.

4. Add water. Bring to a boil.

5. Simmer for 40 minutes with the cover on.

6. Add thickening and stir for 2 minutes.

SAVORY CHICKEN WITH EGGS

SERVES 4 to 6   METHOD: Stewing

INGREDIENTS

2½ to 3 lb chicken, cut into
  6 or 8 pieces
1½ cups water
6 whole eggs, hard-cooked and
  shelled

CONDIMENTS

See Condiments, Savory Chicken,
  page 90
Increase soy sauce to ¾ cup

METHOD

Follow Steps 1 through 4, Savory Chicken, page 90.

5. Simmer for 20 minutes with the cover on.

6. Add hard-cooked eggs; cook 20 minutes on low heat with cover on.

SAVORY CHICKEN WITH CELERY CABBAGE

SERVES 4 to 6   METHOD: Stewing

INGREDIENTS

2½ to 3 lb chicken, cut into
  6 or 8 pieces
1½ cups water
4 cups celery cabbage cut in
  1-inch pieces

CONDIMENTS

See Condiments, Savory Chicken,
  page 90

METHOD

Follow Steps 1 through 4, Savory Chicken, page 90.

5. Simmer for 30 minutes with the cover on.

6. Add celery cabbage; cook 10 minutes on low heat with the cover on.

SAVORY CHICKEN WITH BAMBOO SHOOTS

SERVES 4 to 6   METHOD: Stewing

INGREDIENTS   **CONDIMENTS**

2½ to 3 lb chicken, cut into   *See* Condiments, Savory Chicken,
  6 or 8 pieces   page 90
1½ cups water
4 stalks bamboo shoots, fresh or
  canned, cut in 1-inch pieces

METHOD

Follow Steps 1 through 4, Savory Chicken, page 90.

5. Simmer for 20 minutes with the cover on.

6. Add bamboo shoots; cook 20 minutes on low heat with the cover on.

SAVORY CHICKEN WITH CHESTNUTS

SERVES 4 to 6   METHOD: Stewing

INGREDIENTS   **CONDIMENTS**

2½ to 3 lb chicken, cut into   *See* Condiments, Savory Chicken,
  6 or 8 pieces   page 90
1½ cups water   Increase soy sauce to 1 cup
½ lb chestnuts

METHOD

Put chestnuts in boiling water in a deep pan. Boil for 30 minutes. Allow to cool and shell.

Follow Steps 1 through 4, Savory Chicken, page 90.

5. Simmer for 20 minutes with cover on.

6. Add chestnuts; cook 20 minutes with the cover on.

SAVORY CHICKEN WITH MUSHROOMS

SERVES 4 to 6   METHOD: Stewing

INGREDIENTS

2½ to 3 lb chicken, cut into
  6 or 8 pieces
1½ cups water
1 cup dried whole mushrooms

CONDIMENTS

See Condiments, Savory Chicken,
  page 90
Increase soy sauce to 1 cup

METHOD

Follow Steps 1 through 4, Savory Chicken, page 90.

5. Simmer for 30 minutes with the cover on.

6. Add mushrooms; cook 10 minutes on low heat with the cover on.

SAVORY CHICKEN WITH STRING BEANS

SERVES 4 to 6   METHOD: Stewing

INGREDIENTS

2½ to 3 lb chicken, cut into
  6 or 8 pieces
1½ cups water
½ lb string beans, wash and
  cut off ends

CONDIMENTS

See Condiments, Savory Chicken,
  page 90
Increase soy sauce to 1 cup

METHOD

Follow Steps 1 through 4, Savory Chicken, page 90.

5. Simmer for 20 minutes with the cover on.

6. Add string beans; cook 15-20 minutes with the cover on.

SAVORY DUCK

SERVES 4 to 6   METHOD: Stewing

INGREDIENTS   **CONDIMENTS**

3 to 3½ lb duck, cut into   ⎧ 1 cup soy sauce
  6 or 8 pieces   Mix ⎨ 2 Tbs dry sherry
2 cups water   Sauce ⎨ 2 Tbs brown sugar
                                       ⎩ 1 tsp salt

1 Tbs cornstarch ⎤ Mix
2 Tbs water   ⎦ Thickening   2½ Tbs peanut oil for frying
                                      3 scallions or one medium
                                         onion, stripped
                                      2 cloves garlic, crushed
                                      2 thin slices ginger

METHOD

1. Heat deep pan (350°). Add oil. Quick fry duck until golden brown.
2. Drain excess oil. Add scallions, garlic, and ginger, and quick fry with duck for 2 minutes.
3. Add sauce and mix well with duck.
4. Add water. Bring to boil.
5. Simmer for 2½ hours in a covered pan.
6. Add thickening and stir for 2 minutes.

SAVORY DUCK WITH EGGS

SERVES 4 to 6   METHOD: Stewing

INGREDIENTS   **CONDIMENTS**

3 to 3½ lb duck, cut into   *See* Condiments, Savory Duck,
  6 or 8 pieces   above
2 cups water
6 eggs, hard-cooked and shelled,
  keep eggs whole

METHOD

Follow Steps 1 through 4, Savory Duck, page 94.

5. Simmer for 1½ hours in a covered pan.
6. Add hard-cooked eggs; cook for 30 minutes on low heat with the cover on.

SAVORY DUCK WITH CELERY CABBAGE

SERVES 4 to 6

METHOD: Stewing

INGREDIENTS

3 to 3½ lb duck, cut into
  6 or 8 pieces
2 cups water
4 cups celery cabbage, cut in
  1-inch pieces

CONDIMENTS

See Condiments, Savory Duck,
  page 94

METHOD

Follow Steps 1 through 4, Savory Duck, page 94.

5. Simmer for 1½ hours with the cover on.
6. Add celery cabbage; cook for 30 minutes on low heat with the cover on.

SAVORY DUCK WITH BAMBOO SHOOTS

SERVES 4 to 6

METHOD: Stewing

INGREDIENTS

3 to 3½ lb duck, cut into
  6 or 8 pieces
2 cups water
4 stalks bamboo shoots cut in
  1-inch squares

CONDIMENTS

See Condiments, Savory Duck,
  page 94

METHOD

Follow Steps 1 through 4, Savory Duck, page 94.

5. Simmer for 1½ hours with the cover on.
6. Add bamboo shoots; cook for 25 minutes on low heat with the cover on.

SAVORY DUCK WITH CHESTNUTS

SERVES 4 to 6

METHOD: Stewing

INGREDIENTS

3 to 3½ lb duck, cut into
  6 or 8 pieces
2 cups water
1 lb chestnuts

CONDIMENTS

See Condiments, Savory Duck,
  page 94

METHOD

Put chestnuts in boiling water in deep pan. Boil 30 minutes. Allow chestnuts to cool and shell.

Follow Steps 1 through 4, Savory Duck, page 94.

5. Simmer for 1½ hours with the cover on.
6. Add chestnuts; cook for 30 minutes on low heat with the cover on.

SAVORY DUCK WITH MUSHROOMS

SERVES 4 to 6

METHOD: Stewing

INGREDIENTS

3 to 3½ lb duck, cut into
  6 to 8 pieces
2 cups water
1 cup dried whole mushrooms

CONDIMENTS

See Condiments, Savory Duck,
  page 94

METHOD

Follow Steps 1 through 4, Savory Duck, page 94.

5. Simmer for 1½ hours with the cover on.
6. Add mushrooms; cook for 30 minutes on low heat with the cover on.

SAVORY DUCK WITH STRING BEANS

SERVES 4 to 6

INGREDIENTS

3 to 3½ lb duck, cut into
  6 or 8 pieces
2 cups water
½ lb string beans,
  wash and cut ends

METHOD: Stewing

CONDIMENTS

See Condiments, Savory Duck,
  page 94

METHOD

Follow Steps 1 through 4, Savory Duck, page 94.

5. Simmer for 1 hour and 45 minutes with the cover on.
6. Add string beans; cook for 15-20 minutes with the cover on.

SAVORY PORK

SERVES 4 to 6

INGREDIENTS

2 lb lean pork, cut in 1½-inch
  squares
3 cups water

METHOD: Stewing

CONDIMENTS

Mix Sauce
{
1 cup soy sauce
2 Tbs dry sherry
2 Tbs brown sugar
1 tsp salt
}

2 Tbs peanut oil for frying
3 scallions or ½ medium dry
  onion, stripped
2 cloves garlic, crushed
2 thin slices ginger

METHOD

1. Heat deep pan (350°). Add oil. Quick fry pork until golden brown.
2. Drain excess oil. Add scallions, garlic, and ginger, and quick fry with pork for 2 minutes.
3. Add sauce and mix well with pork.
4. Add water. Bring to a boil.
5. Simmer for 1½ hours with cover on.

NOTE: Savory pork without vegetables may be prepared a day in advance. It may be poured in a square mold and served *en gelée* sliced as hors d'oeuvres. If this dish is to be served *en gelée*, longer cooking (up to 3 hours) is necessary.

SAVORY PORK WITH EGGS

SERVES 4 to 6   METHOD: Stewing

INGREDIENTS

2 lb lean pork, cut in
  1½-inch squares
3 cups water
6 eggs, hard-cooked and shelled

CONDIMENTS

See Condiments, Savory Pork,
  page 97

METHOD

Follow Steps 1 through 4, Savory Pork, page 97.

5. Simmer for 1 hour with the cover on.
6. Add hard-cooked eggs; cook for 30 minutes on low heat, with the cover on.

SAVORY PORK WITH CELERY CABBAGE

SERVES 4 to 6   METHOD: Stewing

INGREDIENTS

2 lb lean pork,
  cut in 1½-inch squares
3 cups water
4 cups celery cabbage, cut in
  1-inch pieces

CONDIMENTS

See Condiments, Savory Pork,
  page 97

METHOD

Follow Steps 1 through 4, Savory Pork, page 97.

5. Simmer for 1 hour and 10 minutes with the cover on.
6. Add celery cabbage; cook for 20 minutes on low heat, with the cover on.

SAVORY PORK WITH BAMBOO SHOOTS

SERVES 4 to 6   METHOD: Stewing

INGREDIENTS   **CONDIMENTS**

2 lb lean pork, cut in   *See* Condiments, Savory Pork,
 1½-inch squares   page 97

3 cups water

4 stalks bamboo shoots, cut in
 1-inch squares

METHOD

Follow Steps 1 through 4, Savory Pork, page 97.

5. Simmer for 1 hour and 10 minutes with the cover on.
6. Add bamboo shoots; cook for 20 minutes on low heat, with the cover on.

SAVORY PORK WITH CHESTNUTS

SERVES 4 to 6   METHOD: Stewing

INGREDIENTS   **CONDIMENTS**

2 lb lean pork, cut in   *See* Condiments, Savory Pork,
 1½-inch squares   page 97

3 cups water

½ lb chestnuts

METHOD

Put chestnuts in boiling water in a deep pan. Boil for 30 minutes. Allow to cool and shell.

Follow Steps 1 through 4, Savory Pork, page 97.

5. Simmer for 1 hour with cover on.
6. Add chestnuts; cook for 30 minutes on low heat, with the cover on.

SAVORY PORK WITH MUSHROOMS

SERVES 4 to 6   METHOD: Stewing

INGREDIENTS   CONDIMENTS

2 lb lean pork, cut in   *See* Condiments, Savory Pork,
  1½-inch squares   page 97
3 cups water
1 cup dried whole mushrooms

METHOD

Follow Steps 1 through 4, Savory Pork, page 97.

5. Simmer for 1 hour and 20 minutes with the cover on.
6. Add mushrooms; cook for 15 minutes on low heat, with the cover on.

SAVORY PORK WITH STRING BEANS

SERVES 4 to 6   METHOD: Stewing

INGREDIENTS   CONDIMENTS

2 lb lean pork, cut in   *See* Condiments, Savory Pork,
  1½-inch squares   page 97
3 cups water
½ lb string beans, wash and
  cut ends

METHOD

Follow Steps 1 through 4, Savory Pork, page 97.

5. Simmer for 1 hour and 10 minutes with the cover on.
6. Add string beans; cook for 15-20 minutes with the cover on.

SAVORY BEEF

SERVES 4 to 6   METHOD: Stewing

INGREDIENTS

2 lb lean beef, cut in 1½-inch squares

3 cups water

CONDIMENTS

Mix Sauce
{
1 cup soy sauce
2 Tbs dry sherry
2 Tbs brown sugar
1 tsp salt
}

2 Tbs peanut oil for frying
3 scallions or ½ medium dry onion, stripped
2 cloves garlic, crushed
2 thin slices ginger
2 cloves or seeds of anise (may be crushed before using)

METHOD

1. Heat deep pan (350°). Add oil. Quick fry beef until brown.
2. Drain excess oil. Add scallions, garlic, anise and ginger, and quick fry with beef for 2 minutes.
3. Add sauce and mix well with beef.
4. Add water. Bring to a boil.
5. Simmer for 3 hours with the cover on.

NOTE: Savory Beef without vegetables may be prepared a day in advance. It may be put in a square mold and served *en gelée* sliced as hors d'oeuvres. It may be made early in the day, allowed to simmer unwatched on a very low heat in a tightly covered pan, cooled and then reheated for dinner.

SAVORY BEEF WITH EGGS

SERVES 4 to 6   METHOD: Stewing

INGREDIENTS

2 lb lean beef, cut in
  1½-inch squares
3 cups water
6 eggs, hard-cooked and shelled,
  keep eggs whole

CONDIMENTS

See Condiments, Savory Beef,
  page 101
Omit cloves or seeds of anise

METHOD

Follow Steps 1 through 4, Savory Beef, page 101.
5. Simmer for 2 hours and 30 minutes with the cover on.
6. Add hard-cooked eggs; cook for 30 minutes on low heat with the
   cover on.

SAVORY BEEF WITH CELERY CABBAGE

SERVES 4 to 6   METHOD: Stewing

INGREDIENTS

2 lb lean beef, cut in
  1½-inch squares
3 cups water
4 cups celery cabbage, cut in
  1-inch pieces

CONDIMENTS

See Condiments, Savory Beef,
  page 101
Omit cloves or seeds of anise

METHOD

Follow Steps 1 through 4, Savory Beef, page 101.
5. Simmer for 2 hours and 40 minutes with the cover on.
6. Add celery cabbage; cook for 20 minutes on low heat with the cover
   on.

SAVORY BEEF WITH BAMBOO SHOOTS

SERVES 4 to 6   METHOD: Stewing

INGREDIENTS   **CONDIMENTS**

2 lb lean beef, cut in   *See* Condiments, Savory Beef,
  1½-inch squares   page 101
3 cups water   Omit cloves or seeds of anise
4 stalks bamboo shoots, cut in
  1-inch squares

METHOD

Follow Steps 1 through 4, Savory Beef, page 101.
5. Simmer for 2 hours and 40 minutes with the cover on.
6. Add bamboo shoots; cook for 20 minutes on low heat with the cover
  on.

SAVORY BEEF WITH CHESTNUTS

SERVES 4 to 6   METHOD: Stewing

INGREDIENTS   **CONDIMENTS**

2 lb lean beef, cut in   *See* Condiments, Savory Beef,
  1½-inch squares   page 101
3 cups water   Omit cloves or seeds of anise
½ lb chestnuts

METHOD

Put chestnuts in boiling water in a deep pan. Boil for 30 minutes. Cool
and shell.
Follow Steps 1 through 4, Savory Beef, page 101.
5. Simmer for 2 hours and 30 minutes with the cover on.
6. Add chestnuts; cook for 30 minutes on low heat with the cover on.

SAVORY BEEF WITH MUSHROOMS

SERVES 4 to 6   METHOD: Stewing

INGREDIENTS

2 lb lean beef, cut in
   1½-inch squares

3 cups water

1 cup dried whole mushrooms

CONDIMENTS

See Condiments, Savory Beef,
   page 101

Omit cloves or seeds of anise

METHOD

Follow Steps 1 through 4, Savory Beef, page 101.

5. Simmer for 2 hours and 40 minutes with the cover on.

6. Add mushrooms; cook for 20 minutes on low heat with the cover on.

SAVORY BEEF WITH STRING BEANS

SERVES 4 to 6   METHOD: Stewing

INGREDIENTS

2 lb lean beef, cut in
   1½-inch squares

3 cups water

½ lb string beans, wash and
   cut ends

CONDIMENTS

See Condiments, Savory Beef,
   page 101

Omit cloves or seeds of anise

METHOD

Follow Steps 1 through 4, Savory Beef, page 101.

5. Simmer for 2 hours and 40 minutes with the cover on.

6. Add string beans, and cook for 15-20 minutes with the cover on.

SAVORY BEEF WITH CARROTS

SERVES 4 to 6   METHOD: Stewing

INGREDIENTS   **CONDIMENTS**

2 lb lean beef, cut in   *See* Condiments, Savory Beef,
  1½-inch squares   page 101
3 cups water   Omit cloves or seeds of anise
4 carrots, cut on the diagonal
  in 1-inch pieces

METHOD

Follow Steps 1 through 4, Savory Beef, page 101.
5. Simmer for 2 hours and 30 minutes with the cover on.
6. Add carrots, and cook for 30 minutes on low heat with the cover on.

FIVE FRAGRANT LAMB
(FLAVOR-ROAST LAMB)

SERVES 4 to 6   METHOD: Stewing

INGREDIENTS   **CONDIMENTS**

3 lb lamb, cut in
  1½-inch squares

Mix Sauce:
- 1 cup soy sauce
- 2 Tbs dry sherry
- 2 Tbs brown sugar
- 1 tsp salt
- ¼ tsp pepper

3 cups water

2 Tbs peanut oil for frying
3 scallions or ½ medium
  onion, stripped
2 cloves garlic, crushed
2 thin slices ginger
2 cloves or seeds of anise
  (may be crushed before
  using)

METHOD

1. Heat deep pan (350°). Add oil. Quick fry lamb until golden brown.
2. Drain excess oil. Add scallions, garlic, cloves or seeds of anise, and ginger, and quick fry with lamb for 2 minutes.
3. Add sauce and mix well with lamb.
4. Add water. Bring to a boil.
5. Simmer for 2 hours with the cover on.

CHAO

The following dishes are cooked according to the *Chao* method. It is the most simple and yet the most difficult of the traditional Chinese cooking methods. The difficulty lies in the correct timing, correct proportions and the correct heat. We have given the correct proportions, but in spite of our effort the correct heat and timing cannot be standardized because it varies with the pan which is used and the stirring technique of the cook. Chinese cooks use a very high heat for *Chao* dishes, but we have lowered the heat somewhat for our American readers. The general rule is to use the highest heat you can cope with. *Keep your mind on the stirring.* If you don't want to be so diligent, you can use a lower heat. Chinese cooks always stay on top of *Chao* dishes, since they can be ruined in minutes. When cooking by this method, it is absolutely essential to have all the ingredients on hand before you set the pan on the fire.

FRIED CHICKEN WITH BAMBOO SHOOTS

SERVES 4 to 6   METHOD: Hot frying

INGREDIENTS   CONDIMENTS

½ lb chicken breast, stripped

2 cups bamboo shoots, stripped

Mix Sauce:
- 3 Tbs soy sauce
- 1 Tbs dry sherry
- ⅛ tsp MSG
- 1 tsp cornstarch

3 Tbs peanut oil for frying

1 clove garlic, crushed

1 scallion, cut in 1-inch strips

1 slice ginger, stripped

METHOD

1. Heat frying pan (350°). Add oil, heat thoroughly.
2. Quick fry scallion, garlic, and ginger for 1 minute.
3. Quick fry chicken for 5 minutes or until moderately brown.
4. Add bamboo shoots, mix thoroughly, and quick fry for 2 minutes, stirring constantly.
5. Add sauce, and quick fry for 2 minutes.

FRIED CHICKEN WITH WATER CHESTNUTS

SERVES 4 to 6   METHOD: Hot frying

INGREDIENTS   CONDIMENTS

½ lb chicken breast, stripped   *See* Condiments, Fried Chicken
1 small can water chestnuts,   with Bamboo Shoots, page 106
 drained and sliced thin

METHOD

Follow Steps 1 through 3, Fried Chicken with Bamboo Shoots, page 106.
4. Add water chestnuts, mix thoroughly, and quick fry 2 minutes, stirring constantly.
5. Add sauce, and quick fry for 2 minutes.

FRIED CHICKEN WITH MUSHROOMS

SERVES 4 to 6   METHOD: Hot frying

INGREDIENTS   CONDIMENTS

½ lb chicken breast, stripped   *See* Condiments, Fried Chicken
¼ lb mushrooms sliced or   with Bamboo Shoots, page 106
 whole, depending on size

METHOD

Follow Steps 1 through 3, Fried Chicken with Bamboo Shoots, page 106.
4. Add mushrooms, mix thoroughly, and quick fry 2 minutes, stirring constantly.
5. Add sauce, and quick fry for 2 minutes.

FRIED CHICKEN WITH CELERY CABBAGE

SERVES 4 to 6   METHOD: Hot frying

INGREDIENTS   **CONDIMENTS**

½ lb chicken breast, stripped   *See* Condiments, Fried Chicken
3 cups celery cabbage, stripped   with Bamboo Shoots, page 106

METHOD

Follow Steps 1 through 3, Fried Chicken with Bamboo Shoots, page 106.

4. Add celery cabbage, mix thoroughly, and quick fry for 2 minutes, stirring constantly.

5. Add sauce, and quick fry for 2 minutes.

FRIED CHICKEN WITH BEAN SPROUTS

SERVES 4 to 6   METHOD: Hot frying

INGREDIENTS   **CONDIMENTS**

½ lb chicken breast, stripped   *See* Condiments, Fried Chicken
3 cups bean sprouts   with Bamboo Shoots, page 106

METHOD

Put bean sprouts in colander, scald with boiling water, and drain.

Follow Steps 1 through 3, Fried Chicken with Bamboo Shoots, page 106.

4. Add bean sprouts, mix thoroughly, and quick fry 2 minutes, stirring constantly.

5. Add sauce, and quick fry for 2 minutes.

FRIED CHICKEN WITH CELERY

SERVES 4 to 6   METHOD: Hot frying

INGREDIENTS

½ lb chicken breast, stripped
3 cups celery, cut in
   1-inch strips

CONDIMENTS

See Condiments, Fried Chicken
with Bamboo Shoots, page 106

METHOD

Boil celery for 2 minutes, drain, and let dry.
Follow Steps 1 through 3, Fried Chicken with Bamboo Shoots, page 106.
4. Add celery, mix thoroughly, and quick fry for 2 minutes, stirring
   constantly.
5. Add sauce, and quick fry for 2 minutes.

CHICKEN OR TURKEY WITH SNOW PEAS

SERVES 4 to 6   METHOD: Hot frying

INGREDIENTS

½ lb uncooked chicken or
   turkey, cut in thin strips
2 cups snow peas
1 cup bamboo shoots, cut in
   strips
1 cup water chestnuts, sliced
   thin

1 Tbs cornstarch ⎱ Mix
2 Tbs water   ⎰ Thickening

CONDIMENTS

Mix
Sauce
⎰
2 to 3 Tbs soy sauce
1 Tbs sherry
½ tsp sugar
1 tsp salt
⅛ tsp MSG
pinch of pepper

4 Tbs peanut oil for frying
2 green onions or
   ½ dry onion, cut in strips
2 cloves garlic, crushed
1 small slice ginger or a
   pinch of garlic powder

METHOD

1. Heat pan (350°). Add 3 Tbs oil, heat thoroughly.
2. Fry garlic, onions, and ginger until light golden brown.
3. Add fowl, and quick fry for 4 minutes. Remove from pan and set aside on a plate.
4. Add remaining Tbs of oil. Add vegetables, and quick fry for 2 minutes.
5. Add fowl and sauce. Stir for 1 minute. Add thickening, and stir for 1 minute.

WALNUT OR ALMOND CHICKEN (TURKEY OR DUCK)

SERVES 4 to 6   METHOD: Hot frying

INGREDIENTS

1½ lb chicken breast (turkey or duck), sliced thin as possible
1 cup walnuts or almond, shredded
½ cup cooked ham, shredded

CONDIMENTS

Mix Sauce { 1½ Tbs soy sauce
2 Tbs dry sherry
½ tsp sugar
½ Tbs salt

3 Tbs peanut oil for frying
2 scallions or ½ medium-size onion, diced
1 thin slice ginger

METHOD

1. Heat skillet (350°). Add oil, heat thoroughly.
2. Quick fry scallions and ginger for 1 minute.
3. Add chicken (tuckey or duck) and ham. Stir constantly for 4 minutes, until almost done.

4. Add sauce, and quick fry for 2 minutes.
5. Add walnuts or almonds; stir for 1 minute, blending thoroughly.

WALNUTS OR ALMONDS WITH WILD GAME
(SUCH AS PHEASANT)

SERVES 4 to 6   METHOD: Hot frying

INGREDIENTS   **CONDIMENTS**

½ lb wild game,
  sliced thin as possible in shreds
1 cup walnuts or almonds,
  shredded
½ cup cooked ham, shredded

Mix Sauce {
1½ Tbs soy sauce
2 Tbs dry sherry
½ tsp sugar
½ tsp salt
1 tsp pepper
}

3 Tbs peanut oil for frying
2 scallions or ½ medium-
  size onion, diced
1 thin slice ginger

METHOD

1. Heat skillet (350°). Add oil, heat thoroughly.
2. Quick fry scallions and ginger for 1 minute.
3. Add wild game and ham. Stir constantly for 4 minutes, or until almost done.
4. Add sauce, and quick fry for 2 minutes.
5. Add walnuts or almonds; stir for one minute, blending thoroughly.

(NOTE: In the following *Chao* recipes using pork, be sure the pork is cut *very* fine for thorough cooking.)

PORK WITH BAMBOO SHOOTS

SERVES 4 to 6   METHOD: Hot frying

INGREDIENTS

½ lb pork, stripped
2 cups bamboo shoots, stripped

CONDIMENTS

Mix
Sauce
{
3 Tbs soy sauce
1 Tbs dry sherry
⅛ tsp MSG
1 tsp cornstarch
}

3 Tbs peanut oil for frying
1 clove garlic, crushed
1 scallion, cut in 1-inch
  strips
1 slice ginger, stripped

METHOD

1. Heat frying pan (350°). Add oil, heat thoroughly.
2. Quick fry scallions, garlic, and ginger for 1 minute.
3. Quick fry pork for 10 minutes or until moderately brown.
4. Add bamboo shoots, mix thoroughly, and quick fry for 2 minutes, stirring constantly.
5. Add sauce, and quick fry for 2 minutes.

PORK WITH WATER CHESTNUTS

SERVES 4 to 6   METHOD: Hot frying

INGREDIENTS

½ lb pork, stripped
1 small can water chestnuts,
  drained and sliced thin

CONDIMENTS

See Condiments, Pork with Bamboo
Shoots, above

METHOD

Follow Steps 1 through 3, Pork with Bamboo Shoots, page 112.

4. Add water chestnuts, mix thoroughly, and quick fry for 2 minutes, stirring constantly.
5. Add sauce, and quick fry for 2 minutes.

PORK WITH MUSHROOMS

SERVES 4 to 6   METHOD: Hot frying

INGREDIENTS

½ lb pork, stripped
¼ lb mushroom, whole or
    sliced, depending on size

CONDIMENTS

See Condiments, Pork with Bamboo Shoots, page 112

METHOD

Follow Steps 1 through 3, Pork with Bamboo Shoots, page 112.

4. Add mushrooms, mix thoroughly, and quick fry for 2 minutes, stirring constantly.
5. Add sauce, and quick fry for 2 minutes.

PORK WITH CELERY CABBAGE

SERVES 4 to 6   METHOD: Hot frying

INGREDIENTS

½ lb pork, stripped
1 lb celery cabbage, shredded

CONDIMENTS

See Condiments, Pork with Bamboo Shoots, page 112

METHOD

Follow Steps 1 through 3, Pork with Bamboo Shoots, page 112.

4. Add celery cabbage, mix thoroughly, and quick fry for 2 minutes, stirring constantly.
5. Add sauce, and quick fry for 2 minutes.

PORK WITH BEAN SPROUTS

SERVES 4 to 6   METHOD: Hot frying

INGREDIENTS   **CONDIMENTS**

½ lb pork, stripped   *See* Condiments, Pork with Bamboo

1 lb bean sprouts   Shoots, page 112

METHOD

Put bean sprouts in colander, scald with boiling water, and drain.

Follow Steps 1 through 3, Pork with Bamboo Shoots, page 112.

4. Add bean sprouts, mix thoroughly, and quick dry for 2 minutes, stirring constantly.

5. Add sauce, and quick fry for 2 minutes.

PORK WITH CELERY

SERVES 4 to 6   METHOD: Hot frying

INGREDIENTS   **CONDIMENTS**

½ lb pork, stripped   *See* Condiments, Pork with Bamboo

2 cups celery, cut in 1-inch   Shoots, page 112
  strips

METHOD

Boil celery for 2 minutes. Drain thoroughly.

Follow Steps 1 through 3, Pork with Bamboo Shoots, page 112.

4. Add celery, mix thoroughly, and quick fry for 2 minutes, stirring constantly.

5. Add sauce, and quick fry for 2 minutes.

BEEF WITH CELERY

SERVES 4 to 6   METHOD: Hot frying

INGREDIENTS   CONDIMENTS

½ lb lean beef, sliced thin as
  possible in strips   ⎧ 1½ Tbs soy sauce
2 cups celery, parboiled,   Mix ⎨ 2 Tbs dry sherry
  drained, and cut in strips   Sauce ⎨ ½ tsp sugar
                                             ⎩ ½ Tbs salt

                                   3 Tbs peanut oil for frying
                                   2 scallions or ½ medium-
                                     size dry onion, diced
                                   1 thin slice ginger

METHOD

1. Heat skillet (350°). Add oil, heat thoroughly.
2. Quick fry scallions and ginger for 1 minute.
3. Add beef. Stir constantly for 4 minutes or until almost done.
4. Add sauce, quick fry until well mixed.
5. Add celery; stir for 4 minutes, blending thoroughly.

BEEF WITH BAMBOO SHOOTS

SERVES 4 to 6   METHOD: Hot frying

INGREDIENTS   CONDIMENTS

½ lb lean beef, stripped   ⎧ 3 Tbs soy sauce
2 cups bamboo shoots, stripped   Mix ⎨ 1 Tbs dry sherry
                                   Sauce ⎨ ⅛ tsp MSG
                                             ⎩ 1 tsp cornstarch

                                   3 Tbs peanut oil for frying
                                   1 clove garlic, stripped
                                   1 scallion, cut in 1-inch
                                     strips
                                   1 slice ginger, stripped

METHOD

1. Heat skillet (350°). Add oil, heat thoroughly.
2. Quick fry scallion, garlic, and ginger for 1 minute.
3. Quick fry beef for 4 minutes or until moderately brown.
4. Add bamboo shoots, mix thoroughly, and quick fry for 4 minutes, stirring constantly.
5. Add sauce, and quick fry for 2 minutes.

BEEF WITH WATER CHESTNUTS

SERVES 4 to 6   METHOD: Hot frying

INGREDIENTS

½ lb beef, stripped

1 small can water chestnuts, drained and sliced thin

CONDIMENTS

See Condiments, Beef with Bamboo Shoots, page 115

METHOD

Follow Steps 1 through 3, Beef with Bamboo Shoots, page 115.

4. Add water chestnuts, mix thoroughly, and quick fry for 2 minutes, stirring constantly.
5. Add sauce, and quick fry for 2 minutes.

BEEF WITH MUSHROOMS

SERVES 4 to 6   METHOD: Hot frying

INGREDIENTS

½ lb beef, stripped

¼ lb mushrooms, whole or sliced, depending on size

CONDIMENTS

See Condiments, Beef with Bamboo Shoots, page 115

METHOD

Follow Steps 1 through 3, Beef with Bamboo Shoots, page 115.

4. Add mushrooms, mix thoroughly, and quick fry for 2 minutes, stirring constantly.
5. Add sauce, and quick fry for 2 minutes.

BEEF WITH CELERY CABBAGE

SERVES 4 to 6

METHOD: Hot frying

INGREDIENTS

½ lb beef, stripped
4 cups celery cabbage, shredded

CONDIMENTS

See Condiments, Beef with Bamboo Shoots, page 115

METHOD

Follow Steps 1 through 3, Beef with Bamboo Shoots, page 115.

4. Add celery cabbage, mix thoroughly, and quick fry for 3 minutes, stirring constantly.
5. Add sauce, and quick fry for 2 minutes.

BEEF WITH BEAN SPROUTS

SERVES 4 to 6

METHOD: Hot frying

INGREDIENTS

½ lb lean beef, stripped
1 lb bean sprouts

CONDIMENTS

See Condiments, Beef with Bamboo Shoots, page 115

METHOD

Put bean sprouts in colander, scald with boiling water, and drain.
Follow Steps 1 through 3, Beef with Bamboo Shoots, page 115.

4. Add bean sprouts, mix thoroughly, and fry 2 minutes, stirring constantly.
5. Add sauce, and quick fry for 2 minutes.

FISH WITH MANDARIN SAUCE

SERVES 4 to 6   METHOD: Hot frying and stewing

This is a classic Chinese recipe for cooking fish. Soy sauce, wine, garlic, and scallions are the traditional accompaniments for fish, since these condiments eliminate fishiness. Any white fish such as cod, halibut, trout, red snapper, sole, bullhead, or dogfish may be used with the same recipe.

INGREDIENTS

2 lb fish fillets, cut in pieces
   2 inches by 3 inches
2 Tbs cornstarch
1 bamboo shoot, stripped,
   (optional)
6 mushrooms, cut in strips
1 cup chicken stock

CONDIMENTS

Mix Sauce
{
½ cup soy sauce
2 Tbs sherry
1 Tbs brown sugar
1 tsp salt
}

4 Tbs peanut oil for frying
1 scallion or ½ medium
   sized dry onion, stripped
2 cloves garlic, crushed
1 slice ginger, stripped

METHOD

1. Coat fish with cornstarch.
2. Heat pan (325°). Add oil, heat thoroughly.
3. Fry fish on both sides until golden brown. Remove from pan.
4. Quick fry scallion, garlic, and ginger until golden brown, stirring constantly.
5. Add mushrooms and bamboo shoots, and quick fry for 1 minute.
6. Add sauce and chicken stock. Bring to a boil. Add fish.
7. Lower heat. Simmer for 15 minutes with the cover on.

SWEET-SOUR FISH

SERVES 4 to 6   METHOD: Hot frying and simmering

INGREDIENTS   **CONDIMENTS**

2 lb fish fillets, cut in pieces
   2 inches by 3 inches
2 Tbs cornstarch

Mix Sweet-Sour Sauce:
- 3 Tbs soy sauce
- 2 Tbs sherry
- 1 cup brown sugar
- 4 Tbs vinegar
- 1 tsp salt
- 2 Tbs cornstarch
- 1 cup chicken stock or water

4 Tbs peanut oil for frying
1 scallion or ½ medium
   sized dry onion, stripped
3 cloves garlic, crushed
1 slice ginger, cut in strips

METHOD

1. Coat fish with cornstarch.

2. Heat frying pan (350°). Add oil, heat thoroughly.

3. Fry fish on both sides until golden brown. Remove from pan.

4. Quick fry scallion, garlic, and ginger until golden brown.

5. Add sweet-sour sauce. Bring to a boil. Stir constantly until thick. Reduce the heat to low.

6. Lower the fish into the sauce. Simmer for 1 minute. Serve hot.

FRIED SHRIMP BALLS

SERVES 4 to 6   METHOD: Deep frying

INGREDIENTS   CONDIMENTS

2 lb fresh shrimp, shelled,
  deveined, and minced
8 water chestnuts, chopped fine
  (available in cans)
2 eggs
1 small scallion or ½ onion,
  choppedfine

Mix
Sauce
{
dash ginger powder
1 tsp salt
3 Tbs dry sherry
1 Tbs water
1 Tbs cornstarch
1 tsp sesame oil or
    peanut oil
pinch of pepper
}

oil for deep frying

METHOD

1. Mix above ingredients and condiments well, and shape into balls
   1 inch in diameter. Add more cornstarch if necessary.
2. Deep fry until golden brown.

MANDARIN FRIED SHRIMP

SERVES 4 to 6   METHOD: Hot frying

INGREDIENTS   CONDIMENTS

1 lb fresh shrimp

Mix
Sauce
{
2 Tbs soy sauce
¼ tsp MSG
1 Tbs cornstarch
3 Tbs water
}

4 Tbs peanut oil for frying
2 small pieces of ginger,
  minced
1 small clove garlic,
  crushed
2 Tbs dry sherry

METHOD

1. Soak shrimp for 10 minutes in bowl of cold water with 1 Tbs of salt. Shell and devein. Dry each shrimp thoroughly with paper towel. Cut in small pieces, about ¾ inch long.
2. Heat skillet (350°). Add oil, heat thoroughly.
3. Quick fry ginger and garlic until golden brown.
4. Add shrimp, quick fry slightly. Add sherry.
5. Add sauce, and quick fry for 2 minutes.

MANDARIN FRIED SHRIMP WITH GREEN PEAS

SERVES 4 to 6

METHOD: Hot frying

INGREDIENTS

1 lb fresh shrimp
1 pkg frozen green peas, defrosted

CONDIMENTS

Mix Sauce
{
2 Tbs soy sauce
¼ tsp MSG
1 Tbs cornstarch
3 Tbs water
}

4 Tbs peanut oil for frying
2 small pieces of ginger, minced
1 small clove garlic, crushed
2 Tbs dry sherry

METHOD

1. Soak shrimp for 10 minutes in bowl of cold water with 1 Tbs of salt. Shell and devein. Dry each shrimp thoroughly with paper towel. Cut in small pieces, about ¾ inch long.
2. Heat skillet (350°). Add oil, heat thoroughly.
3. Quick fry ginger and garlic until golden brown.
4. Quick fry shrimp for 2 to 3 minutes. Add sherry.
5. Add green peas, quick fry for 5 minutes.
6. Add sauce, and quick fry for 2 minutes.

MANDARIN FRIED SHRIMP WITH WATER CHESTNUTS

SERVES 4 to 6   METHOD: Hot frying

INGREDIENTS

1 lb fresh shrimp
1 small can water chestnuts,
  drained

CONDIMENTS

See Condiments, Mandarin Fried
Shrimp with Green Peas, page 121

METHOD

Follow Steps 1 through 4, Mandarin Fried Shrimp with Green Peas,
page 121.

5. Add water chestnuts, quick fry for 4 minutes.
6. Add sauce and quick fry for 2 minutes.

MANDARIN FRIED SHRIMP WITH BAMBOO SHOOTS

SERVES 4 to 6   METHOD: Hot frying

INGREDIENTS

1 lb uncooked shrimp
1 small can bamboo shoots,
  drained and cut in
  ¾-inch lengths

CONDIMENTS

See Condiments, Mandarin Fried
Shrimp with Green Peas, page 121

METHOD

Follow Steps 1 through 4, Mandarin Fried Shrimp with Green Peas,
page 121.

5. Add bamboo shoots, quick fry for 8 minutes.
6. Add sauce, and quick fry for 2 minutes.

MANDARIN FRIED SHRIMP WITH CELERY CABBAGE

SERVES 4 to 6   METHOD: Hot frying

INGREDIENTS

½ lb fresh shrimp, shelled,
  deveined, and diced
4 cups celery cabbage, stripped

CONDIMENTS

Mix Sauce
- 3 Tbs soy sauce
- 1 Tbs dry sherry
- ⅛ tsp MSG
- 1 tsp cornstarch

3 Tbs peanut oil for frying
1 clove garlic, crushed
1 scallion, cut in 1-inch
    strips
1 slice ginger, stripped

METHOD

1. Heat frying pan (350°). Add oil, heat thoroughly.
2. Quick fry scallion, garlic, and ginger for 1 minute.
3. Quick fry shrimp for 5 minutes or until moderately brown.
4. Add Chinese cabbage, mix thoroughly, and quick fry for 2 minutes, stirring constantly.
5. Add sauce, and quick fry for 2 minutes.

MANDARIN FRIED SHRIMP WITH MUSHROOMS

SERVES 4 to 6   METHOD: Hot frying

INGREDIENTS   **CONDIMENTS**

½ lb fresh shrimp, shelled,   *See* Condiments, Mandarin Fried
    deveined, and diced   Shrimp with Celery Cabbage,
¼ lb mushrooms whole or sliced,   page 122
    depending on size

METHOD

Follow Steps 1 through 3, Mandarin Fried Shrimp with Celery Cabbage, page 122.

4. Add mushrooms, mix thoroughly, and quick fry for 2 minutes, stirring constantly.
5. Add sauce, and quick fry for 2 minutes.

MANDARIN FRIED SHRIMP WITH BEAN SPROUTS

SERVES 4 to 6   METHOD: Hot frying

INGREDIENTS   **CONDIMENTS**

½ lb fresh shrimp, shelled,   *See* Condiments, Mandarin Fried
    deveined, and diced   Shrimp with Celery Cabbage,
1 lb bean sprouts   page 122

METHOD

Put bean sprouts in colander, scald with boiling water, and drain.
Follow Steps 1 through 3, Mandarin Fried Shrimp with Celery Cabbage, page 122.

4. Add bean sprouts, mix thoroughly, and quick fry for 2 minutes, stirring constantly.
5. Add sauce, and quick fry for 2 minutes.

CABBAGE HEART WITH CRAB

SERVE 4 to 6   METHOD: Hot frying

INGREDIENTS   **CONDIMENTS**

½ lb crabmeat
1 lb heart of cabbage, shredded

Mix Sauce
{ 1 Tbs soy sauce
  1 Tbs sherry
  1 tsp salt

½ cup chicken stock ⎱ Mix
1 Tbs cornstarch   ⎰ Thickening

3 Tbs corn oil for frying
1 scallion or ½ dry onion, stripped

METHOD

1. Parboil cabbage for 3 minutes. Drain quickly in a colander, and rinse in cold water.
2. Heat pan until hot. Add oil, heat thoroughly.
3. Quick fry scallion until golden brown.
4. Add crab, quick fry for 2 minutes.
5. Add cabbage, cook for 4 minutes.
6. Add sauce. Mix well. Add stock mixture and cook for 2 minutes.

CRAB CUSTARD

SERVES 4 to 6   METHOD: Steaming

INGREDIENTS   **CONDIMENTS**

½ lb crabmeat   1 tsp salt
6 eggs, well-beaten   ⅛ tsp of MSG
1 scallion, chopped fine   1 tsp sesame oil or peanut oil
1 cup water

METHOD

1. Mix well in bowl all ingredients, condiments, and water.
2. Put in top of double boiler over boiling water. Cover top of double boiler. (This dish may also be steamed by placing the bowl on the rack of the steamer.)
3. Cook on a low heat to the consistency of custard.
4. Serve over rice in bowls.

BARBECUED PORK

SERVES 4 to 6   METHOD: Roasting

INGREDIENTS   **CONDIMENTS**

3 lb boneless pork shoulder

		1 cup soy sauce
		½ cup sherry
		½ cup brown sugar
Mix		1 tsp salt
Sauce		⅛ tsp pepper
		⅛ tsp MSG
		1 medium dry onion, diced
		2 cloves garlic, crushed

METHOD

1. Marinate pork in sauce for 2-3 hours. (You may shorten this time to ¼ hour or lengthen it to 4 hours.)
2. Put pork in baking pan* with sauce. Roast in preheated 400° oven for 10 minutes.
3. Lower heat to 275°, and continue to roast for 1 hour and 40 minutes, or until done.
4. Serve hot as an entree.

* The pork should be on a raised broiling pan with a drip pan underneath so it will be roasted and not simmered. Line the drip pan with aluminum foil or it will be hard to clean.

CHAPTER 10

Chinese Food with an American Touch

WHEN the Chinese came to America in the 19th Century during the gold rush days, they began a new chapter in the history of the Oriental culinary arts. The line between authentic Chinese food and its adaptations will become increasingly nebulous, since the future of the art now rests with the overseas Chinese in the United States, southeastern Asia, Formosa, Hawaii, the Philippines and some parts of Europe.

We can look forward to a fruitful collaboration in cookery between East and West and to many exciting combinations of foods as we learn each other's culinary ways. Purists may object to this internationalization of Chinese cooking and may lament that the only result will be a lowering of quality. We believe, however, that it is the continuing creativity, adaptability, and popularity of Chinese cooking which makes it a particularly vital and thriving art today. Any art which looks solely to the past is already dead; we must honor our great classic dishes, but we must not forget that there are Chinese cooks today who are composing recipes which will be the classics of tomorrow.

The Chinese who came to the United States to build the railroads and to dig for gold introduced Chinese cooking to the American taste. Since the majority of these people were from Canton, the Americans first became familiar with the popular versions of Cantonese food. The famous Chop Suey was a variation of a Cantonese dish known as Sub Gum.

There are as many different stories about the birth of Chop Suey as there are varieties of that dish. The name of the dish is rather unfortunate, since it is a kind of pidgin English: "chop" in English meaning to cut, and "suey" in Cantonese meaning hash. One of the stories about the origin of the dish is this: the venerable Viceroy Li Hung Chang was visited by friends late one night when he was the Chinese envoy in Washington. They were quite ravenous, and Mr. Li was embarrassed to find that his cupboard was bare; he asked his cook to put together any odds and ends he could find. The guests were so hungry that they ate the food with delight. When they asked the name of the wonderful dish, the Viceroy christened it Chop Suey. Thirty years ago in Chinese restaurants the dish was known as Li Hung Chang Chop Suey.

All over the world, with the exception of China, Chop Suey is known as a Chinese dish. Although it originated in America, the basic idea of the dish is Chinese—the combination of meat and vegetables, the cutting, and the thickening with cornstarch. Once the reader understands the philosophy of Chinese cooking, she can realize the reasons why Chop Suey falls below the standard of culinary correctness and what can be done to save it. We believe that the dish has possibilities, and that it should be improved rather than abolished.

The greatest fault is that most versions of the dish are not true to the proper cooking method. It is a *Chao* dish in conception, and, as we know, *Chao* or hot fried dishes are supposed to have crisp vegetables and a clear, pure, and smooth sauce. They must be prepared quickly and served immediately. The dish should not be left on the stove to dissolve itself into a stew. Furthermore, the good Chinese dishes have proportion, standard, and dominance, whereas in the usual version of Chop Suey anything goes.

Chop Suey can be a delicious dish if it is prepared in the proper manner. We have renovated the recipe in conformity with the principles of the Chinese culinary art, and we think you will enjoy it.

CHICKEN CHOP SUEY

SERVES 4 to 6   METHOD: Hot frying

INGREDIENTS

½ lb chicken breast, stripped
¼ lb celery cabbage, stripped
¼ lb bamboo shoots, stripped,
    or ¼ lb bean sprouts

1 Tbs cornstarch ⎤ Mix
2 Tbs water ⎦ Thickening

CONDIMENTS

Mix
Sauce ⎰ 2 to 3 Tbs soy sauce
1 Tbs sherry
½ tsp sugar
1 tsp salt
⅛ tsp MSG
pinch of pepper

4 Tbs peanut oil for frying
2 scallions or 1 dry onion,
    stripped
2 cloves garlic, crushed
1 small ginger slice or a
    pinch of ginger powder

METHOD

1. Prepare fresh vegetables according to charts on pages 197-199. Drain and dry thoroughly.

2. Heat skillet (350°). Add 3 Tbs oil, heat thoroughly.

3. Quick fry garlic, scallions, and ginger until light golden brown.

4. Add chicken; quick fry for 4 minutes. Remove from pan and set aside.

5. Add remaining Tbs of oil. Add vegetables; quick fry for 3 minutes. Add chicken and sauce, stir evenly; 1 minute.

6. Add thickening; stir constantly for 1 minute.

BEEF CHOP SUEY

SERVES 4 to 6

METHOD: Hot frying

INGREDIENTS

½ lb lean beef, stripped
¼ lb celery, cut in 1-inch
  strips
¼ lb bean sprouts
¼ lb broccoli or cabbage, stripped

1 Tbs cornstarch ⎫ Mix
2 Tbs water ⎬ Thickening

CONDIMENTS

See Condiments, Chicken Chop
Suey, page 128

METHOD

Follow Steps 1 through 3, Chicken Chop Suey, page 128.
4. Add beef; quick fry for 4 minutes. Remove from pan and set aside.
5. Add remaining Tbs of oil. Add vegetables; quick fry for 3 minutes.
   Add beef and sauce; stir evenly for 1 minute.
6. Add thickening; stir constantly for 1 minute.

PORK CHOP SUEY I

SERVES 4 to 6

METHOD: Hot frying

INGREDIENTS

½ lb pork, stripped
¼ lb bamboo shoots, stripped
¼ lb water chestnuts, sliced
  thin

1 Tbs cornstarch ⎫ Mix
2 Tbs water ⎬ Thickening

CONDIMENTS

See Condiments, Chicken Chop
Suey, page 128

METHOD

Follow Steps 1 through 3, Chicken Chop Suey, page 128.

4. Add pork; quick fry for 10 minutes. Remove from pan and set aside.
5. Add remaining Tbs of oil. Add vegetables; quick fry for 2 minutes. Add pork and sauce; stir evenly for 1 minute.
6. Add thickening; stir constantly for 1 minute.

PORK CHOP SUEY II

SERVES 4 to 6   METHOD: Hot frying

INGREDIENTS   **CONDIMENTS**

½ lb pork, stripped   *See* Condiments, Chicken Chop
¼ lb heart of cabbage, stripped   Suey, page 128
1 medium dry onion, stripped

1 Tbs cornstarch ⎱ Mix
2 Tbs water   ⎰ Thickening

METHOD

Follow Steps 1 through 3, Chicken Chop Suey, page 128.

4. Add pork; quick fry for 10 minutes. Remove from pan and set aside.
5. Add remaining Tbs of oil. Add vegetables; quick fry for 2 minutes. Add pork and sauce; stir evenly for 1 minute.
6. Add thickening; stir constantly for 1 minute.

TURKEY CHOP SUEY

SERVES 4 to 6   METHOD: Hot frying

INGREDIENTS   **CONDIMENTS**

½ lb white meat of turkey,   *See* Condiments, Chicken Chop
   stripped   Suey, page 128
½ cup celery, stripped
½ cup bean sprouts

1 Tbs cornstarch ⎱ Mix
2 Tbs water   ⎰ Thickening

METHOD

Follow Steps 1 through 3, Chicken Chop Suey, page 128.

4. Add turkey; quick fry for 8 minutes. Remove from pan and set aside.
5. Add remaining Tbs of oil. Add vegetables; quick fry for 2 minutes. Add turkey and sauce; stir evenly for 1 minute.
6. Add thickening; stir constantly for 1 minute.

SHRIMP CHOP SUEY

SERVES 4 to 6   METHOD: Hot frying

INGREDIENTS

½ lb fresh shrimp, shelled,
  deveined, and diced
1 cup fresh green peas
1 cup botton mushrooms or
  coarsely chopped large
  mushrooms

1 Tbs cornstarch ⎫
2 Tbs water   ⎬ Mix
                   ⎭

CONDIMENTS

See Condiments, Chicken Chop
Suey, page 128

METHOD

Follow Steps 1 through 3, Chicken Chop Suey, page 128.

4. Add shrimp; quick fry for 4 minutes. Remove from pan and set aside.
5. Add remaining Tbs of oil. Add vegetables; quick fry for 2 minutes. Add shrimp and sauce; stir evenly 1 minute.
6. Add thickening; stir constantly for 1 minute.

SHRIMP AND CHICKEN CHOP SUEY

SERVES 4 to 6

METHOD: Hot frying

INGREDIENTS

CONDIMENTS

¼ lb chicken breast, diced
¼ lb fresh shrimp, deveined,
  shelled, and diced
1 cup fresh green peas
1 cup button mushrooms or
  coarsely chopped large
  mushrooms

See Condiments, Chicken Chop
Suey, page 128

1 Tbs cornstarch ⎫ Mix
2 Tbs water   ⎰ Thickening

METHOD

Follow Steps 1 through 3, Chicken Chop Suey, page 128.
4. Add chicken and shrimp; quick fry for 4 minutes. Remove from pan
   and set aside.
5. Add remaining Tbs of oil. Add vegetables; quick fry for 2 minutes.
   Add chicken, shrimp, and sauce; stir evenly for 1 minute.
6. Add thickening; stir constantly for 1 minute.

SHRIMP AND PORK CHOP SUEY

SERVES 4 to 6

METHOD: Hot frying

INGREDIENTS

CONDIMENTS

¼ lb fresh shrimp, shelled,
  deveined, and stripped
¼ lb pork, stripped
½ cup bean sprouts
½ cup bamboo shoots, stripped

See Condiments, Chicken Chop
Suey, page 128

1 Tbs cornstarch ⎫ Mix
2 Tbs water   ⎰ Thickening

METHOD

Follow Steps 1 through 3, Chicken Chop Suey, page 128.

4. Add shrimp and pork; quick fry for 10 minutes. Remove from pan and set aside.

5. Add remaining Tbs of oil. Add vegetables; quick fry for 2 minutes. Add shrimp, pork and sauce; stir evenly for 1 minute.

6. Add thickening; stir constantly for 1 minute.

SUB GUM

SERVES 4 to 6   METHOD: Hot frying

Sub Gum was the Cantonese ancestor of Chop Suey. It is similar to its offspring in many ways. However, Chop Suey usually contains only one kind of meat, whereas Sub Gum contains two or more. The name Sub Gum means "Many Precious Things."

INGREDIENTS

¼ lb fresh shrimp, shelled, deveined, and stripped
¼ lb chicken breasts, stripped
¼ lb pork, stripped
¼ lb cooked ham, stripped
½ cup bamboo shoots, stripped
½ cup water chestnuts, stripped
½ cup bean sprouts

1 tsp cornstarch ⎱ Mix
1 Tbs water   ⎰ Thickening

CONDIMENTS

Mix Sauce ⎰ 2 Tbs soy sauce
1 Tbs sherry
½ tsp sugar
½ tsp salt
⅛ tsp MSG
dash pepper

2 Tbs peanut oil for frying
2 scallions or 1 dry onion, stripped
1 clove garlic, crushed
1 ginger, sliced thin

METHOD

1. Heat skillet (375°). Add oil, heat thoroughly.
2. Quick fry scallions, garlic, and ginger until light golden brown.
3. Add pork; hot fry for 8 minutes.
4. Add chicken, ham, and shrimp; hot fry for 3 minutes.
5. Add vegetables. Mix well, and fry for 3 minutes.
6. Add thickening; stir for 2 minutes.

CHICKEN FOO YUNG

SERVES 4 to 6   METHOD: Sautéing

INGREDIENTS

CONDIMENTS

¼ lb chicken breast, diced
   very thin
1 cup button mushrooms or
   coarsely chopped large
   mushrooms
6 eggs
3 Tbs cornstarch

1 tsp salt
⅛ tsp MSG
⅛ tsp pepper
1 dry onion, diced

6 Tbs peanut oil for frying

METHOD

1. Beat eggs; slowly add cornstarch. Beat well.
2. Add all ingredients and condiments. Mix thoroughly.
3. Heat skillet (300°). Add oil, heat thoroughly.
4. Pour mixture into pan a little at a time, to make small pancakes, 3
   inches in diameter.
5. Cook until almost "set," as you would a pancake.
6. Turn over and cook other side.

CHICKEN AND HAM FOO YUNG

SERVES 4 to 6   METHOD: Sautéing

INGREDIENTS   **CONDIMENTS**

¼ lb chicken breast, stripped   *See* Condiments, Chicken Foo
  very thin   Yung, page 134
¼ lb cooked ham, stripped
6 eggs
3 Tbs cornstarch

METHOD

Follow Steps 1 through 6, Chicken Foo Yung, page 134.

PORK FOO YUNG

SERVES 4 to 6   METHOD: Sautéing

INGREDIENTS   **CONDIMENTS**

¼ lb cooked pork, stripped   *See* Condiments, Chicken Foo
1 cup bean sprouts   Yung, page 134
6 eggs
3 Tbs cornstarch

METHOD

Follow Steps 1 through 6, Chicken Foo Yung, page 134.

SHRIMP FOO YUNG

SERVES 4 to 6   METHOD: Sautéing

INGREDIENTS   **CONDIMENTS**

¼ lb fresh shrimp,   *See* Condiments, Chicken Foo
  shelled, deveined, and diced   Yung, page 134
1 cup button or whole
  mushrooms, diced
3 eggs
3 Tbs cornstarch

METHOD

Follow Steps 1 through 6, Chicken Foo Yung, page 134.

CRAB FOO YUNG WITH BEAN SPROUTS

SERVES 4 to 6

METHOD: Sautéing

INGREDIENTS
¼ lb crabmeat
1 cup bean sprouts
6 eggs
3 Tbs cornstarch

CONDIMENTS
See Condiments, Chicken Foo Yung, page 134

METHOD

Follow Steps 1 through 6, Chicken Foo Yung, page 134.

CRAB FOO YUNG WITH BAMBOO SHOOTS

SERVES 4 to 6

METHOD: Sautéing

INGREDIENTS
¼ lb fresh crabmeat
1 cup bamboo shoots, stripped
6 eggs
3 Tbs cornstarch

CONDIMENTS
See Condiments, Chicken Foo Yung, page 134

METHOD

Follow Steps 1 through 6, Chicken Foo Yung, page 134.

CRAB FOO YUNG WITH MUSHROOMS

SERVES 4 to 6   METHOD: Sautéing

INGREDIENTS

¼ lb crabmeat
1 cup mushrooms, stripped
1 cup green peas
6 eggs
3 Tbs cornstarch

CONDIMENTS

See Condiments, Chicken Foo Yung, page 134

METHOD

Follow Steps 1 through 6, Chicken Foo Yung, page 134.

PINEAPPLE SPARERIBS

SERVES 4 to 6   METHOD: Simmering and baking

INGREDIENTS

2 lb spareribs, cut in
  2-inch lengths
1 No. 1 can chunk pineapple
Water to barely cover

CONDIMENTS

Mix Sauce
2 Tbs soy sauce
1 Tbs sherry
2 Tbs sugar
1 tsp salt
1 Tbs vinegar
⅛ tsp MSG
1 small slice of ginger, minced

METHOD

1. Simmer spareribs in water for 45 minutes in a covered pan. Drain and dry.
2. Marinate spareribs in sauce for 1 hour or more.
3. Bake in 380° oven for 20 minutes with sauce and juice from pineapple.
4. Add pineapple; bake for 5 minutes.

SWEET AND SOUR SPARERIBS

SERVES 4 to 6   METHOD: Simmering and sautéing

INGREDIENTS   **CONDIMENTS**

2 lb spareribs, cut in
   2-inch lengths
Water to barely cover

Mix Sauce
{
3 Tbs soy sauce
1 Tbs sherry
2 Tbs vinegar
3 Tbs sugar
½ tsp salt
⅛ tsp MSG
1 slice ginger, stripped
3 Tbs cornstarch
}

3 Tbs peanut oil for frying
2 cloves garlic, crushed

METHOD

1. Simmer spareribs in water for 45 minutes. Drain and dry. May be
   left in the refrigerator overnight.
2. Heat skillet (375°). Add oil, heat thoroughly. Add garlic.
3. Add the spareribs, and fry until golden brown.
4. Add the sauce; cook for 5 minutes. Serve hot.

BAKED FISH

SERVES 4 to 6   METHOD: Sautéing and baking

INGREDIENTS   **CONDIMENTS**

2 lb cod, sea bass, or other
   white fish, cut into steaks
1 slice boiled ham, cut into
   1-inch strips
⅛ lb fresh shrimp,
   shelled and deveined

Mix Sauce
{
1 Tbs soy sauce
1 Tbs sherry
1 tsp sugar
1 tsp salt
⅛ tsp MSG
}

4 crisp bacon strips
cornstarch

3 Tbs peanut oil for frying
1 dry onion, stripped
2 cloves of garlic, crushed

METHOD

1. Coat fish with cornstarch.
2. Heat skillet (325°). Add oil, heat thoroughly.
3. Fry onions and garlic for 1 minute or until golden brown.
4. Fry fish until golden brown on both sides.
5. Add sauce; put ham, shrimp and bacon on top of fish.
6. Wrap fish and all other ingredients and condiments in foil, and bake in 300° oven for 15 minutes.

SHRIMP TEMPURA

SERVES 4 to 6

METHOD: Deep frying

INGREDIENTS
1 lb fresh shrimp,
   shelled and deveined
2 eggs, well-beaten

peanut oil for deep frying
(2 inches deep)

2 Tbs flour
2 Tbs cornstarch } Mix Batter
2 Tbs water

METHOD

1. Cut shrimp halfway through on inner curve and spread open to make a butterfly.
2. Add eggs to batter mixture.
3. Heat skillet (350°). Add oil, heat thoroughly.
4. Dip shrimp in batter and egg mixture, and fry until golden brown.

HOT FRIED SHRIMP WITH CROUTONS

SERVES 4 to 6

METHOD: Deep frying and hot
frying

INGREDIENTS

4 cups fresh shrimp, shelled,
deveined, and cut in ½-inch
pieces
8 slices stale bread, cut in
½-inch cubes

CONDIMENTS

Mix
Sauce
{
1 Tbs soy sauce
1 Tbs sherry
1 tsp salt
⅛ tsp MSG
1 tsp cornstarch
1 Tbs water
}

peanut oil for deep frying
(2 inches deep)
2 cloves garlic, crushed
1 small slice ginger,
minced

METHOD

1. Heat skillet (375°). Add oil, heat thoroughly.

2. Deep fry bread cubes until light golden brown.

3. Remove cubes; drain on paper towel.

4. Pour out oil. Save for future use. Return 2 Tbs of oil to skillet.

5. Hot fry garlic and shrimp for 2 minutes.

6. Add sauce. Stir well. Add bread cubes.

SWEET-SOUR SHRIMP WITH CROUTONS

SERVES 4 to 6

METHOD: Deep frying and hot frying

INGREDIENTS

4 cups fresh shrimp, shelled, deveined, and cut in ½-inch pieces

8 slices stale bread, cut in ½ cubes

CONDIMENTS

Mix Sauce
- ½ Tbs soy sauce
- 1 tsp sherry
- 5 Tbs brown sugar
- 5 Tbs vinegar
- 1 tsp salt
- ⅛ tsp MSG
- 1 Tbs cornstarch
- 2 Tbs water

peanut oil for deep frying (2 inches deep)
1 scallion or 1 dry onion
1 garlic clove, crushed
1 ginger, sliced

METHOD

1. Heat skillet (375°). Add oil, heat thoroughly.

2. Deep fry bread cubes until light golden brown.

3. Remove croutons, and drain on paper towel.

4. Pour out excess oil. Save for future use. Return 2 Tbls of oil to skillet.

5. Hot fry shrimp, garlic, ginger, and scallion for 2 minutes.

6. Add sauce. Stir well. Add croutons. Serve immediately.

CHAPTER 11

American Food with a Chinese Touch

IT HAS often been said that many of the happiest discoveries of the kitchen are accidental.

Many of the recipes in this chapter were the result of homesick missionaries and their stubborn Chinese cooks. Missionaries in China learned to appreciate Chinese food. They found that they could eat delicious dishes on their meager stipends, and that the health-giving qualities enabled them to keep up their strength while they worked in the Lord's vineyard. Now and then, however, they would yearn for the food of their native land. By the waters of the Yangtze, the Frenchman would dream of a *pot-au-feu*, while visions of beefsteak and fried chicken would dance in the heads of the Americans.

The American missionary would instruct his cook to broil a steak, medium rare, with mushrooms. The cook, incorrigibly Chinese, would then proceed to cook it in his own fashion—thousands of years of culinary traditions are not tossed off lightly. We can imagine the missionary's chagrin turning to delight as he tasted the new culinary creation. The beefsteak, taken from an elderly cow, would have been transformed by the alchemy of Chinese culinary principles into a cut as tender as a filet.

Occasionally an American missionary would hire a cook who had worked for Europeans, and there would be an even greater exchange of culinary ideas, such as Southern Fried Chicken, by way of Paris, cooked in the style of Peking. The result was a truly international style of cooking. We collected some of these recipes from our missionary friends when we were in China, and we continued to experiment with East-meets-West recipes in the United States.

Mrs. Lee has been experimenting in this vein with her students, and we have heard that American husbands and children like their favorite dishes cooked with a light Chinese accent.

Our American friends are intrigued with this style of cookery and apply the Chinese culinary principles to their favorite dishes with results that are often spectacularly good. We hope that our readers will continue the experiment in their own kitchens. The chapter is not closed.

A NOTE ON BROILING

The secret of successful broiling is low heat. The door must be open, or the meat will be baked and not broiled. Use the low setting on the broiler or, if the oven is not equipped with one, place the meat 6 inches from the heat. Remember, in charcoal broiling it is the gray, ashen embers which do the best work—not the fiery red coals. Try to duplicate this conditions in your oven. Broiling on low temperatures takes a longer time than high-heat broiling, so one must be patient. Use a meat thermometer to check the internal temperature.

BEEF TENDERLOIN

SERVES 4 to 6   METHOD: Broiling

INGREDIENTS

2 lb beef tenderloin,
   whole or cut in steaks
6 large mushroom caps

CONDIMENTS

Marinade
- ½ cup sesame oil
- 1 Tbs sherry
- ⅛ tsp MSG
- 3 cloves of crushed garlic

METHOD

1. Marinate tenderloin for 1 to 2 hours. Turn occasionally.
2. Broil gently on one side under a gentle fire.
3. Turn meat over, put mushroom caps on top, and broil on the other side

BEEF STEAK

SERVES 4 to 6   METHOD: Broiling

NOTE: This is a good recipe for steak that tends to be tough; the oil
marinade tenderizes the meat. It is the fat in well-marbled
prime steaks which makes them so tender. Soaking in oil follows this principle. Although many people marinate meat in
soy sauce mixtures, it is not always advisable. If the meat is a
little tough, the soy sauce will make it tougher.

INGREDIENTS   **CONDIMENTS**
2 lb steak   2 cups peanut oil

Mix ⎰1 Tbs soy sauce
Sauce ⎱3 cloves garlic, crushed

METHOD

1. Cut slashes ⅛-inch deep across the grain on both sides.
2. Soak in peanut oil for one hour.
3. Remove from oil. Rub with sauce.
4. Broil gently until done.

A NOTE ON ROASTING

Outdoor Chinese ovens use a very low heat for tenderness. The meat
is usually hung from the top so it will cook in an even, dry heat. To duplicate these conditions in American ovens, use very low heat. In order
to keep the heat dry and even, the meat should rest on as little surface
as possible. If the meat is put in a flat roasting pan, it will stew in its own
juices and become tough. Correct roasting cooks the meat with a dry,
even heat on all sides and keeps the juices where they belong — inside
the meat. The meat should be elevated with a drip pan underneath.
The meat may be hung or speared on a rotisserie; it may rest on prongs,
or on an airy rack. The main principle is to *surround the meat with as
much air as possible, and let it touch as little metal as possible.*

In roasting, the juices of the meat should be sealed in. The cornstarch mixture which we use in some of the following recipes is used for this purpose. Another method is to use a very high heat in the first few minutes of roasting to form a crust. Roast meat should be crisp on the outside and juicy on the inside.

ROAST PORK

SERVES 4 to 6   METHOD: Roasting

INGREDIENTS   **CONDIMENTS**

2 to 3 lb rolled
  shoulder of pork

Coating
- 4 Tbs soy sauce
- 1 Tbs sherry
- 1 Tbs cornstarch
- ⅛ tsp pepper
- ⅛ tsp MSG
- 2 cloves garlic, crushed

METHOD

1. Preheat oven to 275°.
2. Coat meat with coating mixture. It seals in the juices and makes the meat crisp on the outside and tender and juicy on the inside.
3. Roast in 275° oven until meat thermometer registers 170° (approximately 45 minutes per pound).

SUGAR-ROAST HAM

SERVES 4 to 6   METHOD: Roasting

INGREDIENTS   **CONDIMENTS**

3 to 4 lb ham

Coating
- 2 Tbs soy sauce
- 1 Tbs sherry
- 1 Tbs cornstarch
- 2 Tbs brown sugar
- 1 tsp salt
- ⅛ tsp MSG
- ⅛ tsp pepper
- ¼ tsp ground cloves

METHOD

1. Preheat oven to 275°.

2. Coat meat with coating mixture. It seals in the juices and makes the meat crisp on the outside and tender and juicy on the inside.

3. Roast in 275° oven until meat thermometer registers 170° (approximately 45 minutes per pound).

ROAST BEEF

SERVES 4 to 6   METHOD: Roasting

INGREDIENTS

3 to 4 lb rolled
   sirloin tip roast

CONDIMENTS

Coating
- 4 Tbs soy sauce
- 1 Tbs sherry
- 1 Tbs cornstarch
- ⅛ tsp pepper
- ⅛ tsp MSG
- 3 cloves garlic, crushed

METHOD

1. Preheat oven to 275°.

2. Coat meat with coating mixture. It seals in the juices and makes the meat crisp on the outside and tender and moist on the inside.

3. Roast in 275° oven until meat thermometer registers:
    135° (approximately 50 minutes per pound) for rare
    150° (approximately 60 minutes per pound) for medium
    160° (approximately 70 minutes per pound) for well done

NOTE: The roast may be studded with mushroom caps ½ hour before it is taken out of the oven.

ROAST LAMB

SERVES 4 to 6   METHOD: Roasting

INGREDIENTS   CONDIMENTS

3 to 4 lb roast of lamb

Coating
- 4 Tbs soy sauce
- 2 Tbs sherry
- 1 Tbs cornstarch
- 2 cloves crushed anise
- ⅛ tsp MSG
- 4 cloves garlic, crushed

METHOD

1. Preheat oven to 275°.

2. Coat meat with coating mixture. It seals in the juices and makes the meat crisp on the outside and tender and juicy on the inside.

3. Roast in 275° oven until meat thermometer registers 160° (approximately 45 minutes per pound).

ROAST TURKEY

SERVES 4 to 6   METHOD: Roasting

INGREDIENTS   CONDIMENTS

16 to 18 lb turkey

Marinade
- ⅔ cup soy sauce
- 1 cup sherry
- 1 Tbs sugar
- 1 tsp salt
- 1 tsp MSG
- ⅛ tsp pepper
- 4 cloves of crushed garlic
- 2 Tbs sesame oil

METHOD

1. Wash turkey inside and out. Remove pin feathers.

2. Rub with marinade. Refrigerate overnight.

3. Preheat oven to 400°.

4. Brown turkey in 400° oven for ½ hour.

5. Reduce heat to 300°.

6. Wrap turkey in aluminum foil. Bake at 300° until meat thermometer registers 180° (approximately 15 to 18 minutes per pound).

CHINESE HAMBURGER

SERVES 4 to 6

METHOD: Hot frying or broiling

INGREDIENTS

1 lb ground beef
¼ cup mushrooms, finely chopped
1 cup minced water chestnuts
  (optional)
1 egg
2 Tbs cornstarch

CONDIMENTS

Mix Sauce
{
3 Tbs soy sauce
1 Tbs sherry
¼ tsp salt
⅛ tsp MSG
1 tsp sugar
1 clove minced garlic
1 pinch of ginger powder or one small slice of ginger, minced
}

METHOD

1. Mix all ingredients together in a bowl with exception of cornstarch. Add sauce and mix thoroughly.

2. Sprinkle meat mixture with cornstarch.

3. Form into patties.

4. Broil or fry until done. They may also be charcoal broiled.

SOUTHERN FRIED CHICKEN BY WAY OF SHANTUNG

SERVES 4 to 6   METHOD: Deep frying

INGREDIENTS

3 lb chicken,
  cut in large pieces

2 eggs, beaten

2 Tbs cornstarch ⎤ Mix
2 Tbs water   ⎦ Thickening

CONDIMENTS

Mix
Sauce
⎰ 3 Tbs soy sauce
⎪ 3 Tbs sherry
⎪ 1 tsp sugar
⎪ 1 tsp salt
⎨ ⅛ tsp MSG
⎪ ⅛ tsp pepper
⎪ 1 Tbs sesame oil
⎪ 2 cloves garlic, crushed
⎱ 1 small slice ginger minced

peanut oil to deep fry
(2 inches deep)

METHOD

1. Marinate chicken in sauce for three hours in the refrigerator.
2. Heat skillet. Add oil and heat to 375°.
3. Add beaten eggs to cornstarch mixture.
4. Dip chicken pieces into batter.
5. Deep fry until golden brown.

LIVER AND ONIONS

SERVES 4 to 6   METHOD: Hot frying

INGREDIENTS

1 lb liver, sliced thin in
  1-inch pieces

8 scallions, cut in 1½-inch
  lengths, (use part of the tops
  for color)

cornstarch

CONDIMENTS

Mix
Sauce
⎰ 3 Tbs soy sauce
⎪ 1 Tbs sherry
⎨ 1 tsp sugar
⎱ ½ tsp salt

5 Tbs peanut oil for frying
1 clove of garlic, crushed
1 pinch of ginger powder

METHOD

Slice the liver in thin pieces 1 inch long. It will slice easier if it is semi-frozen.

1. Dry liver. Coat thoroughly with cornstarch.
2. Heat skillet. Add oil and heat to 375°.
3. Hot fry garlic for 1 minute.
4. Add liver, and quick fry for 3 minutes. Sprinkle with ginger powder.
5. Add scallions, and quick fry for 2 minutes.
6. Add sauce, and quick fry for 1 minute.

CHARCOAL GRILLED LAMB CHOPS

SERVES 4 to 6   METHOD: Broiling

INGREDIENTS

12 lamb chops

CONDIMENTS

Marinade
{
1 cup soy sauce
½ cup sherry
1 tsp sesame oil
½ tsp salt
⅛ tsp MSG
⅛ tsp pepper
2 cloves garlic, crushed
5 scallions cut in strips
}

METHOD

1. Grease grill of a charcoal broiler or hibachi. Light charcoal and wait until the coals are gray and ashen.
2. Trim excess fat from the chops. Marinate for 15 minutes.
3. Grill over coals until done. (The grill should not be too close to the coals nor should the coals be very hot. Low steady heat produces the best results. The chops will cook slowly and remain tender and juicy.)

CHAPTER 12

$\mathcal{S}$pecialties

Just as each province has its own specialties and even a small village may have become known for an especially delightful dish, every Chinese cook has his own special preparations which are the basis for his reputation. In this chapter, we will limit ourselves to three main kinds of specialties: banquet foods, Nomadic dishes, and the authors' specialties.

The Great Banquet Dishes

This section is especially for gourmets and food hunters. A trip to the strange and mysterious Chinese market will be necessary for most of the recipes. These are the "big" dishes which are served in feasts all over China; they are the prestige dishes, and their appearance on the table is the high point of a many-course dinner.

The recipe for the authentic Peking Duck appears in this chapter. The incomparable flavor of the duck is a result of the vapors of the wine, soy sauce, and other condiments penetrating the meat; if the duck were simply soaked in the marinade, it would become slightly tough. Peking Duck is not difficult to prepare, and the authors believe it will become a favorite of American gourmets.

Sea cucumber, birds' nest, sharks' fin, fish lips, and fish tripe dishes are only for those who are willing to take a dare. They are the Chinese equivalents of caviar and *pâté de foie gras*, truffles, and sweetbreads, and are celestial foods to the Chinese gourmets. These items should be bought "treated" or "cured"; otherwise, a whole season can be spent getting them ready for the table.

We must give warning that some of these exotic dishes are expensive and difficult to prepare. The authors have found, however, that Americans enjoy them after they have overcome their initial hesitancy.

PEKING DUCK I

(This is the original, authentic version of this famous dish.)

SERVES 4 to 6   METHOD: Roasting

INGREDIENTS   **CONDIMENTS**

1 fresh, drawn duck, head and neck on

Mix Sauce
- 1 cup soy sauce
- ½ cup sherry
- 6 Tbs brown sugar
- 1 Tbs salt
- ⅛ tsp pepper
- 3 scallions, diced
- 3 cloves garlic, crushed

METHOD

1. Make a shallow cut on the side of the neck, ⅛ inch deep, and ½ inch long.
2. Insert a paper straw and blow the bird up until it is swollen. (The point of this operation is to separate the skin from the meat so that the meat will be tender and the skin crisp.) The air is blown underneath the skin, not into any body cavity.
3. Sew neck opening so air does not escape.
4. Put duck in a colander and pour boiling water over it until the skin is almost white. Hang in an unheated oven overnight to dry.°
5. In the afternoon before party, take the duck down, fill body cavity with sauce, and resew the opening. Reserve some sauce for basting.
6. Preheat oven to 300°. Hang duck in oven again and roast for 2½ to 3 hours. Baste occasionally.

° To hang duck, put one rack on the highest ledge of oven. Remove any unnecessary racks. Put a foil-lined drip pan underneath duck. You may hang the duck by the neck with a hook, a string, or a skewer-and-string arrangement.

PEKING DUCK II

SERVES 4 to 6   METHOD: Simmering and deep frying

INGREDIENTS   **CONDIMENTS**

1 Long Island duck,
  whole and drawn
Boiling water

Mix Sauce
- 1 cup soy sauce
- ½ cup sherry
- 6 Tbs brown sugar
- 1 Tbs salt
- ⅛ tsp pepper
- 3 scallions, diced
- 3 cloves of garlic, crushed

METHOD

1. To duck and sauce, add enough boiling water almost to cover. Cover tightly. Simmer until almost done (approximately 1 hour). The duck may also be precooked by steaming; this is the traditional Chinese method of preparing duck for frying. Place duck and sauce in a bowl on the steamer rack, and cook until almost done.
2. Dry overnight. It must be thoroughly dry, or the dish will not not be successful.
3. Before duck is to be served, heat 3 inches of oil to 375°, and brown duck on both sides. This process will only take a few minutes. (The combination of precooking and deep-frying produces a very succulent duck which is crisp on the outside and tender on the inside.)

SHARKS' FIN

SERVES 4 to 6   METHOD: Stewing

INGREDIENTS   **CONDIMENTS**

1 lb treated sharks' fin
3 cups water
3 cups chicken stock
4 whole chicken breasts
½ lb ham, whole

Mix Sauce
- 3 Tbs soy sauce
- 3 Tbs sherry
- 1 Tbs sugar
- ⅛ tsp MSG
- ⅛ tsp pepper
- 2 tsp sesame oil

1 tsp cornstarch ⎤ Mix
1 Tbs water   ⎦ Thickening

2 scallions, diced
2 garlic cloves, crushed
4 slices ginger, stripped

METHOD

Preparation: Wash treated sharks' fin in cold water and soak for 3 hours, until softened. Change water and wash again. Drain.

1. Boil sharks' fin in water with ginger for 1 hour in a covered pan.
2. Drain, add chicken stock, and bring to a boil.
3. Add chicken, ham, garlic, and scallions, and again bring to a boil.
4. Simmer for 2 hours in a tightly covered pan. Remove and discard chicken and ham.
5. Add sauce. Cook for ½ hour in a tightly covered pan.
6. Add thickening. Cook for 5 minutes, stirring constantly.

FISH LIPS

SERVES 4 to 6   METHOD: Stewing

INGREDIENTS   ### CONDIMENTS

½ lb treated fish lips
3 cups water
4 cups chicken stock
2 chicken breasts, whole
½ lb ham, whole

Mix Sauce ⎰ 3 Tbs soy sauce
          ⎱ 3 Tbs sherry
            1 Tbs sugar
            ⅛ tsp MSG
            ⅛ tsp pepper

1 tsp cornstarch ⎤ Mix
1 Tbs water   ⎦ Thickening

2 scallions, diced
3 garlic cloves, crushed
6 slices ginger, stripped

METHOD

Preparation: Soak fish lips for seven days, changing water daily.
1. Boil fish lips in water with ginger for 3 hours. Change water twice. Drain and rinse in cold water. Squeeze out excess moisture.

2. Bring chicken stock and water to a boil.

3. Add fish lips, chicken, ham, garlic, and scallions and again bring to a boil.

4. Reduce heat and simmer for 3½ hours in a covered pan.

5. Remove and discard chicken and ham. Add sauce, and cook for ½ hour.

6. Add thickening. Cook for 5 minutes.

FISH TRIPE

SERVES 4 to 6   METHOD: Stewing

INGREDIENTS

½ lb fish tripe, treated
2 chicken breasts
½ lb ham, whole
3 cups chicken stock
3 cups water

1 tsp cornstarch ⎤ Mix
1 Tbs water   ⎦ Thickening

CONDIMENTS

Mix Sauce ⎰ 3 Tbs soy sauce
             3 Tbs sherry
             1 Tbs sugar
             ⅛ tsp MSG
             ⅛ tsp pepper

2 diced scallions
2 garlic cloves, crushed
4 slices ginger, stripped

METHOD

Preparation: Soak fish tripe in hot water for three hours. Wash three times, squeezing out all water.

1. Boil fish tripe in water with ginger for 2 hours. Change water twice. Drain and rinse in cold water. Squeeze out all moisture.

2. Add chicken stock, ham, chicken breasts, garlic, and scallions, and bring to a boil.

3. Simmer for 2 hours in a covered pan. Remove and discard chicken and ham.
4. Add sauce. Cover tightly and cook for ½ hour.
5. Add thickening. Cook for 5 minutes, stirring constantly.

SEA CUCUMBER

SERVES 4 to 6

METHOD: Stewing

INGREDIENTS

1 lb sea cucumber, treated
3 cups water
3 chicken breasts
1 lb ham, whole
3 cups chicken stock

1 tsp cornstarch } Mix
1 Tbs water } Thickening

CONDIMENTS

Mix Sauce:
3 Tbs soy sauce
3 Tbs sherry
1 Tbs sugar
⅛ tsp MSG
⅛ tsp pepper

2 scallions, diced
2 garlic cloves, crushed
4 slices ginger, stripped

METHOD

Preparation: Soak the sea cucumber for 7 days, changing water daily until thoroughly washed.

1. Boil cucumber in water with ginger for 3 hours. Change water twice. Drain and rinse with cold water. Squeeze out excess moisture.
2. Put cucumber, chicken breasts, ham, garlic, and scallions in cold chicken stock, and bring to a boil.
3. Simmer for 2 hours in a tightly covered pan.
4. Remove and discard chicken and ham. Add sauce and cook covered for ½ hour.
5. Add thickening. Cook for 5 minutes, stirring constantly.

BIRDS' NEST CHICKEN SOUP

SERVES 4 to 6   METHOD: Simmering

INGREDIENTS

½ lb dried birds' nests
3 lb whole chicken
1 can chicken stock
2 qts water

1 tsp cornstarch ⎱ Mix
1 Tbs water ⎰ Thickening

CONDIMENTS

2 Tbs sherry
1 Tbs salt
⅛ tsp MSG
2 slices of ginger, cut
in strips

METHOD

1. Soak birds' nests in water for ½ hour. Drain.
2. Put chicken, stock, water, and all condiments into a soup pot.
3. Bring to a boil. Add birds' nests and again bring to a boil.
4. Simmer in a covered pan for 1 hour.
5. Add thickening. Stir for 5 minutes.
6. Serve soup in small bowls. Serve chicken on a platter.

NOMADIC DISHES

Although many people think of China as a homogeneous civilization, there are within China many subcultures, each of which has its own characteristic style of living and its own characteristic diet. The five main races of China are the Han, who are the people of China proper, the Mongolians, the Tibetans, the Manchurians, and the Mohammedan tribes.

Outside the Great Wall are the tribes of the frontier. The Mongols are the superb horsemen who are descendents of the great Kublai Khan, who once controlled an Empire from Peking to Vienna. Many of the barbecued dishes of China had their origin at the campfires of the nomads. Such dishes as the Mongolian Stove from southeastern Asia were taken up by the gourmets of Peking and renovated into festive dishes.

The Mohammedan tribes were principally found in Sinkiang, a remote area in northwest China. Their main contribution to the Chinese cuisine was the introduction of mutton into the Chinese diet. Since they followed the Hebrew dietary laws, they abstained from pork. The Mohammedans adopted many of the classic Chinese dishes and substituted mutton for pork. The gourmets of Peking in turn became interested in some of the Moslem dishes, such as the famous flavor-roast lamb and grilled beef.

GRILLED BEEF OR LAMB

SERVES 4 to 6   METHOD: Barbecuing

INGREDIENTS

4 lb lean beef or lamb,
  sliced paper thin

CONDIMENTS

Marinade
- 2 cups soy sauce
- 2 cups sherry
- 1 tsp sesame oil
- ½ tsp salt
- ⅛ tsp MSG
- ⅛ tsp pepper
- 2 cloves garlic, crushed
- 5 green onions, cut in strips

METHOD

1. Grease grill of hibachi or charcoal broiler. Light charcoal and wait until the coals are gray and ashen.
2. Marinate beef or lamb for 5 minutes.
3. Grill meat piece by piece and eat immediately. (Everyone gathers around the coals and cooks his own food.)

THE MONGOLIAN STOVE

At night on the Asian steppes, the nomadic tribes gathered around their fires and cooked their simple food. They speared chunks of meat and cooked them in primitive cauldrons. Although the gourmets of Peking transformed the Mongolian stove into a very festive party dish, it still appeals to our elemental love of fire, food, and companionship.

The stove is a large copper or aluminum bowl, usually about 15 inches in diameter, with a metal chimney in the center. The chimney burns charcoal, heating the soup and other ingredients which are placed in the bowl. The stove is lighted very much like a charcoal broiler. About 6 lumps of charcoal are placed in the chimney, squirted with lighter fluid, and lighted with a match. The coals are allowed to settle down to a steady even heat before any ingredients are added. There is a cover which fits around the chimney and over the bowl.

The ingredients are arranged attractively on the table in trays or on separate round plates circling the stove. Soup bowls and spoons are also placed on the table.

In the Peking Mongolian stove and the Mongolian Mutton stove, the guests spear their own slices of meat with bamboo sticks or silver cocktail forks and cook them in the boiling broth. The soup may then be served in the bowls.

In the Ten Precious Mongolian Stove and the Chrysanthemum Stove, the hostess adds all the ingredients and condiments to the stove at the table. The guests spear whatever food interests them. The soup is then served.

PEKING MONGOLIAN STOVE

SERVES 4 to 6

INGREDIENTS

2 cups chicken stock
5 cups hot water
3 scallions, sliced in thin strips
6 dry mushrooms, soaked
   and sliced
4 lb lean beef, sliced
   paper thin

CONDIMENTS

2 cloves garlic, crushed
1 slice ginger, diced
1 Tbs salt
⅛ tsp pepper

Mix Dipping Sauce
{ 1 cup soy sauce
¼ cup sherry
⅛ tsp pepper

METHOD

1. Light the Mongolian stove.
2. Mix garlic, ginger, salt and pepper with chicken stock and water. Bring to a boil on the kitchen stove.

3. Fill the Mongolian stove with above hot mixture.
4. Add the scallions and mushrooms, and bring to a boil.
5. The time has now come for the guests to cook the slices of meat in the boiling broth, then to dip them in the sauce. (Sauce is served in individual bowls or saucers.)

MONGOLIAN MUTTON STOVE

SERVES 4 to 6

INGREDIENTS

2 cups canned undiluted
  chicken or turkey stock
5 cups hot water
6 dry mushrooms, soaked
  and sliced
3 scallions, sliced in thin strips
4 lb mutton or lamb,
  sliced paper thin

CONDIMENTS

See Condiments, Peking Mongolian
Stove, page 159

METHOD

Follow Steps 1 through 5, Peking Mongolian Stove, page 159.

TEN PRECIOUS MONGOLIAN STOVE

SERVES 4 to 6

INGREDIENTS

¼ lb chicken breast,
  sliced thin as possible
¼ lb chicken livers,
  sliced thin as possible
¼ lb shelled, deveined shrimp
  sliced thin
¼ lb boned fish, sliced thin

CONDIMENTS

2 Tbs soy sauce
1 Tbs sherry
1 tsp salt
⅛ tsp MSG
⅛ tsp pepper
2 cloves of garlic, crushed
1 diced scallion

½ lb spinach or celery cabbage   1 slice of ginger, diced
  cut in thin strips
3 cups chicken or
  turkey stock, canned
  and undiluted
2 cups water

METHOD

1. Light the Mongolian stove.
2. Bring chicken stock and water to a boil on the kitchen stove.
3. Fill the Mongolian stove with hot stock.
4. Add all ingredients and condiments to the Mongolian stove at the table. (Everything should be arranged attractively. One method is to put the ingredients on separate platters around the stove. Another method is to arrange them in separate piles on a tray.)
5. Simmer until tender, and serve in soup bowls.

CHRYSANTHEMUM STOVE

SERVES 4 to 6

INGREDIENTS

2 cups fresh white
  chrysanthemum petals,
  washed thoroughly
¼ lb chicken breast,
  sliced thin as possible
¼ lb chicken livers, sliced thin
¼ lb shrimp, shelled, deveined,
  and sliced thin
¼ lb precooked ham, shredded
¼ lb spinach or celery
  cabbage, cut in thin strips
3 cups canned undiluted
  chicken or turkey stock
4 cups water

CONDIMENTS

½ cup soy sauce
1 tsp salt
⅛ tsp MSG
⅛ tsp pepper
1 scallion, diced
1 clove of garlic, crushed
1 slice of ginger, diced

METHOD

1. Light the Mongolian stove.
2. Bring chicken stock and water to a boil on the kitchen stove. Fill the Mongolian stove with the hot broth. Bring to a boil.
3. Add all the ingredients and condiments. Bring to a boil again.
4. Serve in soup bowls.

THE AUTHORS' SPECIALTIES

TENDER-CRISP CORNISH GAME HEN OR SQUAB

SERVES 4 to 6

METHOD: Steaming and deep frying

INGREDIENTS

CONDIMENTS

3 whole Cornish game hens or
　6 squab

Marinade
- ½ cup soy sauce
- 1 Tbs sherry
- 1 Tbs brown sugar
- ⅛ tsp MSG
- ⅛ tsp pepper
- 2 slices ginger, stripped

Glaze
- 2 Tbs honey
- 2 Tbs soy sauce

oil for deep frying

METHOD

1. Marinate birds for ½ hour or more.
2. Put birds and marinade in a bowl, and place on the rack of the steamer. Steam for 40 minutes.
3. Dry birds thoroughly. Glaze with honey mixture.
4. Deep fry in 3 inches of oil until golden brown.

TENDER-CRISP PORK

SERVES 4 to 6

METHOD: Simmering and
deep frying

INGREDIENTS
2 lb rolled pork loin
2 cups water
2 Tbs cornstarch
1 egg, beaten

CONDIMENTS
2 Tbs salt
⅛ tsp MSG
⅛ tsp pepper
2 slices ginger
3 cloves of garlic, crushed
2 slices of ginger, diced

peanut oil for deep frying
(about 2 inches deep)

METHOD

1. Bring the water to a boil. Add condiments except oil.
2. Add pork and boil for 5 minutes. Reduce heat and simmer for 1½ hours, covered tightly. Add more water if necessary.
3. Remove pork from water and dry thoroughly.
4. Coat with beaten egg and sprinkle with cornstarch.
5. Heat oil for deep frying (375°). Deep fry pork until golden brown.

DRUNKEN DUCK OR CHICKEN

SERVES 4 to 6

METHOD: Simmering and
marinating

INGREDIENTS
1 whole duck or fryer
water to cover fowl

CONDIMENTS
2 Tbs salt
⅛ tsp MSG
⅛ tsp pepper
1 diced scallion
2 cloves of garlic, crushed

sherry or sauterne to
cover fowl

METHOD

1. Add condiments except wine to water. Bring to a boil.
2. Lower fowl into boiling water.
3. Simmer in a covered pan for ½ hour.
4. Remove fowl from the water. Cool and dry thoroughly in the refrigerator (at least 6 hours).
5. Cut fowl in half. Put in a large jar, cover with wine, and keep in refrigerator for a week. Serve cold.

DRUNKEN PORK

SERVES 4 to 6

METHOD: Simmering and marinating

INGREDIENTS

2 to 3 lb boneless rolled
  pork roast
water to cover roast

CONDIMENTS

2 Tbs salt
⅛ tsp MSG
⅛ tsp pepper
1 scallion, diced
2 cloves of garlic, crushed

sherry or sauterne to
  cover pork

METHOD

1. Add all condiments except wine to water. Bring to a boil.
2. Lower pork into boiling water. It should be whole; if necessary, cut in large pieces.
3. Lower the heat and simmer pork in a tightly covered pan for ½ hour.
4. Remove pork from water. Cool and dry for at least 6 hours in the refrigerator.
5. Place in a large jar, cover with wine, and leave in the refrigerator for a week. (The pork may be cut in large pieces so it will fit into the jar.)

SHERRY CHICKEN

SERVES 4 to 6

METHOD: Sautéing and simmering

INGREDIENTS

3 lb chicken, whole or
cut in large pieces

CONDIMENTS

Mix Sauce
- ½ cup soy sauce
- 2 cups sherry
- 2 Tbs sugar
- 1 tsp salt
- ⅛ tsp MSG
- ⅛ tsp pepper
- 2 cloves of garlic, crushed
- 1 thin slice of ginger, chopped finely or a dash of ginger powder

2 Tbs peanut oil for frying

METHOD

1. Heat skillet on a moderate fire (300°). Add oil, and heat thoroughly.
2. Brown chicken on all sides. Drain off excess oil.
3. Add sauce. Bring to a boil.
4. Boil for 25 minutes in a covered pan.
5. Reduce heat and simmer for 15 minutes.

BANQUET CHICKEN

SERVES 4 to 6

METHOD: Steaming

INGREDIENTS

3 lb chicken, whole or
cut in large pieces
8 dry mushrooms, soaked
18 dry lily flowers, washed
and soaked (optional)

1 tsp cornstarch ⎤ Mix
1 Tbs water ⎦ Thickening

CONDIMENTS

Mix Sauce
- 3 Tbs soy sauce
- 4 Tbs sherry
- 1 tsp sugar
- 1 tsp salt
- ⅛ tsp MSG
- ⅛ tsp pepper
- 3 scallions, diced
- 1 clove of garlic, crushed
- 1 thin slice of ginger, diced

METHOD

1. Place chicken, sauce, lily flowers, and mushrooms in medium-sized bowl.
2. Place bowl on rack of steamer over 2 inches of water (may also be cooked in double boiler).
3. Cover *tightly* and steam for 1½ hours. Replenish water if lid is not air-tight.
4. Add thickening. Stir for 1 minute.

HONEY CHICKEN

SERVES 4 to 6

METHOD: Sautéing and simmering

INGREDIENTS

CONDIMENTS

3 lb chicken, whole or cut in pieces

Mix Sauce
- 2 Tbs soy sauce
- ½ cup sherry
- 2 Tbs honey
- 1 tsp salt
- ⅛ tsp MSG
- 1 scallion, diced
- 1 thin slice of ginger, chopped finely, or a dash of ginger powder

2 Tbs of peanut oil for frying

METHOD

1. Heat skillet on a moderate fire (300°). Add oil, heat thoroughly.
2. Brown chicken on all sides. Drain off excess oil.
3. Slowly pour sauce over chicken.
4. Simmer in a covered pan for ½ hour.

ROAST BEAN CURD

SERVES 4 to 6
INGREDIENTS

2 pieces of bean curd, cut in
  1½″ cubes (Bean curd is
  sold in Chinese markets in
  standard pieces similar
  to cream cheese.
  It should be refrigerated and
  eaten within 2 days.)

METHOD: Quick frying
CONDIMENTS

Mix
Sauce
{
2½ Tbs soy sauce
1 Tbs sherry
½ tsp salt
⅛ tsp sugar
⅛ tsp MSG
⅛ tsp pepper
1 Tbs cornstarch
}

1 scallion, diced, or ½ dry
  onion
1 clove garlic, crushed
3 Tbs peanut oil for frying

METHOD

1. Quick fry scallion and garlic in peanut oil until light golden.
2. Quick fry bean curd on all sides until light golden.
3. Add sauce slowly to bean curd.
4. Lower heat, cover the pan, and simmer for 5 minutes.

CHAPTER 13

Rice Dishes

RICE in China has an almost sacred character. The lives of millions of people are dependent on the rice harvest. For centuries, the pattern of human life in thousands of Chinese villages has been governed by the seasonal rhythms of growing rice, planting and harvesting, fertilizing and flooding. Rice is a product of civilized man; it cannot be grown by the careless and the indifferent. Where there is rice, there is order and discipline, intelligence and planning, patience and tedious labors.

To the Chinese, rice is the symbol of life and fertility. At Chinese weddings, it was the custom to throw the rice on the bridal pair with the wish that they may be blessed with many children.

Although rice is the staple food of millions of Chinese, it is never eaten alone, even by the poorest of the poor. Rice in China is the equivalent of bread in the West—something must go with it. Vegetables are the common, inexpensive food and are usually combined with small amounts of pork, poultry, game, fish, or sea food. The usual evening meal in a Chinese family of average means would consist of rice with a few meat, vegetable, or fish dishes and a soup.

At feasts where there are so many courses and such an impressive array of foods, little rice is served. When rice and salt dishes appear on the table, it is the customary sign that the feast is about to end and that all drinking of wine and beer should cease.

Rice is not the staple food of all of China, however; north of the Yangtze, rice does not grow as abundantly as wheat, barley, and other grains. Noodles, steamed breads, various kinds of pastries, and corn cakes replace rice as the staple food in Northern China, although rice is served at feasts and on other occasions.

In China, there are two main kinds of rice. In addition to the ordinary table rice, there is a sticky, glutinous rice which is used for sweet things. The principal varieties of table rice are the long-grained rice which is preferred in the northern part of China, and the round-grain rice which is preferred in Shanghai and other areas in the middle part of China.

The amount of water which is needed varies with the kind of rice used and the texture which is desired. Round rice takes longer to cook and requires less water than the long-grained rice to produce the same effect. Some people prefer hard rice in the style of the Chop Suey place, and others prefer a softer rice of the sort which is served in China, particularly in the central part of China. If the softer rice is desired, more water is used.

The authors have found in their experiments that long-grained rice and round-grained rice may be happily married. The long grain rice has a fluffy texture, but it is dry and tasteless. The round-grain rice has a good flavor, but it is sticky and soggy. When they are cooked together, the long-grain rice borrows the flavor from its partner and absorbs the excess moisture; thus, each ingredient lends its strength to the other and compensates for the weaknesses of its partner.

There are many ways of cooking rice, and each method has its appropriate technique. Plain rice may be boiled or steamed. In addition, there are various dishes which use rice as their principal ingredient: fried rice, congee, or rice soup, and two kinds of delicious rice casseroles which are new to the West and will be of interest to our readers.

Rice must be washed before it is used in order to remove the excess starch so that it will not be sticky. The Chinese wash their rice in baskets under a stream of water. This method may be duplicated with a fine colander. Wash the rice under the faucet until the water which runs off the rice is almost clear. Another method which some cooks find more convenient is to wash the rice three times in the pan in which it will be cooked. The water should always be cold, of course.

Perfect rice is white, fluffy, and "just right" in texture—neither too hard nor too soft. It is not lumpy or sticky.

There is no mystery in cooking rice properly. It simply requires a certain amount of self restraint. The lid on the pan must be tight, and it must be left on. *Do not stir. Do not peek. Do not lift the lid.* We have found that this is a very difficult rule for most women to follow—the Pandora instinct runs deep. (If one can't stand the suspense, a glass lid will help the cook keep in touch, although many nutritionists discourage this practice on the grounds that light destroys riboflavin.) Remember that it is the steam which cooks the rice—DON'T PEEK.

For boiled rice, which is the method most often used, the water level should be about 1 inch above the level of the rice. The water should be cold.

For boiled rice, the mixture is first brought to a boil on a *high fire,* and is cooked on a high heat for 5 to 7 minutes until most of the water is absorbed. The heat is then turned low, and the rice simmered for 20 to 30 minutes until it is ready to be served. It may simmer on the stove for one or two hours without harm, as long as the heat is very low, the lid is tight, and the pan is left unopened. Steamed rice is cooked on a moderate heat.

Two recipes for the basic preparation of rice follow. The reader will note that the quantity of rice required may seem a bit large. The Chinese often cook a large quantity of rice so that the leftover quantity may be used on subsequent days for other dishes. The reader may substitute as much rice as is needed in either of these recipes. Remember that 1 cup of uncooked rice usually renders 3 cups when cooked.

PLAIN RICE I

SERVES 4 to 6   METHOD: Boiling

3 cups washed, uncooked rice
cold water to cover 1 inch above the
   surface of the rice

METHOD

1. Add the water to the rice in the pan. Be sure the lid fits tightly.
2. Put the pan on a quick fire and bring to a boil; continue to cook on a high fire with the lid on for 5 to 7 minutes. By this time most of the water will have been absorbed.
3. You may now lift the cover ONCE to see if most of the water is gone, but it isn't necessary.
4. Lower the heat and simmer the rice in a covered pan for 20 to 30 minutes. Do not lift the cover until it is ready to be served.

PLAIN RICE II

SERVES 4 to 6   METHOD: Steaming

3 cups of rice
cold water to cover ½ inch above the surface of the rice

METHOD

1. Put rice into top of a large double boiler and wash it three times.
2. Leave water about ½ inch higher than rice. The boiler should be large enough to allow for expansion of rice.
3. Fill bottom of the double boiler with 4 to 5 cups of water. Put double boiler together, cover the top tightly.
4. Cook over moderate heat for 1 to 1½ hours. Do not stir, do not lift the cover.

MEN-FAN (RICE STEW)

SERVES 4 to 6   METHOD: Stewing

INGREDIENTS

2 cups rice
1 chicken breast, shredded
½ cup mushrooms
2 stalks scallion or ½ dry
   onion cut in thin shreds

CONDIMENTS

Mix Sauce
{
4 Tbs soy sauce
1 Tbs sherry
⅓ tsp salt
⅛ tsp MSG
⅛ tsp pepper
}

METHOD

1. Marinate chicken in sauce for 10 minutes.
2. Wash and cook rice according to instructions for plain rice. Cook for ten minutes on high heat in a covered pan, and then interrupt the process. Lift the cover.
3. Pour chicken and sauce on top of the rice. (The water should be almost completely absorbed by this time).
4. Put the cover on again and cook on a low heat for 15 minutes. Turn the heat to very low and simmer for another 10 minutes.

LEFTOVER RICE

If the rice is warmed up properly, it will be like freshly cooked rice. It can be reheated in a fraction of the time which is required for cooking rice. Leftover rice is the basis for fried rice, it may also be used in rice soup.

Rice fried is an excellent way to use any number of oddments in the refrigerator. Various kinds of cooked meat and vegetables may be cut in fine shreds or strips and added to the dish for color and flavor.

Toward the end of the cooking, leftover meat gravy or juice may be added.

Before you put the leftover rice in the refrigerator, let it cool completely and then loosen and separate the grains with a tablespoon, or you will not be able to reheat it properly.

RULES FOR WARMING UP COOKED RICE

1. Add 1 tsp cold water to each cup of cold cooked rice.
2. Loosen the grains with a fork.
3. Heat over a slow fire for 8 to 10 minutes. Cover tightly and let the steam cook the rice until it is hot.

FRIED RICE WITH GREEN PEAS

SERVES 4 to 6   METHOD: Hot frying

INGREDIENTS   **CONDIMENTS**

6 cups cold cooked rice
1 cup or ½ pkg. frozen
  green peas, thawed
3 eggs beaten
2 Tbs cold water to loosen the rice

Mix Sauce
- 3 Tbs soy sauce
- 1 Tbs sherry
- ⅓ tsp salt
- ⅓ tsp MSG
- ⅛ tsp pepper
- 1 Tbs cornstarch

3 Tbs. peanut oil for frying
½ onion, shredded

METHOD

1. Add 2 Tbs of cold water to the cold cooked rice. Loosen and separate the grains.
2. Heat frying pan until it is very hot. Add the oil and heat thoroughly.
3. Fry the onions to light golden brown.
4. Add the eggs and the rice. Cook for 2 minutes, stirring constantly.
5. Add the green peas and mix with the rice and other ingredients. Stir for 3 minutes.
6. Add the sauce and mix thoroughly. Serve hot.

FRIED RICE WITH BEEF AND ONIONS

SERVES 4 to 6   METHOD: Hot frying

INGREDIENTS   **CONDIMENTS**

6 cups cold cooked rice
1 lb cooked beef sliced
  as thin as possible
1 dry onion shredded
  as thin as possible
2 Tbs cold water to loosen the rice

Mix Sauce
- 3 Tbs soy sauce
- 1 Tbs sherry
- ⅓ tsp salt
- ⅓ tsp MSG
- ⅛ tsp pepper
- 1 Tbs cornstarch

3 Tbs. peanut oil for frying

METHOD

1. Add 2 Tbs of cold water to cold cooked rice. Loosen and separate the grains.
2. Marinate beef in sauce for 4 minutes.
3. Heat frying pan until it is very hot (375° or more). Add oil and heat thoroughly.
4. Fry onions to a light golden brown.
5. Add beef with sauce and cook for 2 to 3 minutes stirring constantly.
6. Add rice and mix with the other ingredients. Heat thoroughly. Serve hot.

FRIED RICE WITH HAM

SERVES 4 to 6

METHOD: Hot frying

INGREDIENTS

6 cups cold cooked rice

1 generous cup cooked ham, shredded as thin as possible

2 eggs beaten

2 Tbs cold water to loosen the rice

CONDIMENTS

See Condiments, Fried Rice with Green Peas, page 173

METHOD

1. Add 2 Tbs of cold water to cold cooked rice. Loosen and separate the grains.
2. Marinate ham in sauce for 3 minutes.
3. Heat skillet (375° or more). Add oil and heat thoroughly.
4. Fry onion to a light golden brown.
5. Add ham and sauce. Cook for 2 minutes stirring constantly.
6. Add the rice and the eggs. Mix thoroughly. Serve hot.

FRIED RICE WITH BACON AND EGGS

SERVES 4 to 6   METHOD: Hot frying

INGREDIENTS   **CONDIMENTS**

6 cups cold cooked rice   *See* Condiments, Fried Rice with
½ lb bacon, cut in 1″ strips   Green Peas, page 173
  or diced in small squares
3 eggs beaten
2 Tbs cold water to loosen rice

METHOD

1. Add 2 Tbs of cold water to cold cooked rice. Loosen and separate the grains. Add beaten eggs to bacon in a small bowl and mix well.
2. Heat skillet on a very high fire. Add oil and heat thoroughly.
3. Fry onion and bacon to a light golden brown.
4. Add eggs and cook for 2 minutes, stirring constantly.
5. Add rice and mix with other ingredients.
6. Add sauce and mix with all the ingredients. Heat thoroughly and serve hot.

TEN PRECIOUS FRIED RICE

SERVES 4 to 6   METHOD: Hot frying

INGREDIENTS   **CONDIMENTS**

6 cups cold cooked rice   ⎧ 4 Tbs soy sauce
2 Tbs diced cooked ham   ⎪ 2 Tbs sherry
4 Tbs shredded cooked chicken   Mix ⎨ ⅓ tsp salt
½ cup sliced sausage or bacon   Sauce ⎪ ⅓ tsp MSG
¼ cup cooked shrimp, diced   ⎪ ⅛ tsp pepper
¼ cup frozen green peas   ⎩ 1 Tbs cornstarch
6 canned or fresh mushrooms,
  sliced
2 eggs well beaten   4 Tbs peanut oil for frying
2 Tbs cold water to loosen rice ½ dry onion, shredded

METHOD

1. Add 2 Tbs cold water to rice and loosen the grains as much as possible.
2. Heat frying pan on a high flame (375°); add oil and heat thoroughly.
3. Fry onion, and bacon, or sausage together for 2 minutes, stirring constantly.
4. Add ham, chicken, shrimp, and sauce. Cook for 2 minutes.
5. Add rice and cook for 2 minutes, stirring constantly.
6. Add eggs, mushrooms, and green peas. Stir constantly until all ingredients are thoroughly mixed. Cook for 2 minutes. Serve hot.

FRIED RICE WITH SHRIMP OR CRAB

SERVES 4 to 6   METHOD: Hot frying

INGREDIENTS

6 cups cold cooked rice
½ lb fresh shrimp, shelled,
   deveined and shredded or
½ lb fresh crab, shredded
2 eggs well beaten
2 Tbs cold water to loosen the rice

CONDIMENTS

Mix Sauce
- 4 Tbs soy sauce
- 2 Tbs sherry
- ⅓ tsp salt
- ⅓ tsp MSG
- ⅛ tsp pepper

4 Tbs peanut oil for frying
½ dry onion, shredded

METHOD

1. Add 2 Tbs cold water to rice and loosen the grains as much as possible.
2. Mix shrimp or crab and eggs together in a small bowl.
3. Heat frying pan on a high flame to 375°; add oil and heat thoroughly.
4. Fry onion to a light golden brown.
5. Add shrimp or crab and eggs and cook for 2 minutes stirring constantly.

6. Add rice and cook for 2 minutes, stirring constantly.
7. Add sauce. Stir constantly for 2 minutes until all ingredients are thoroughly mixed.

TEN PRECIOUS RICE CASSEROLE

SERVES 4 to 6   METHOD: Hot frying and simmering

INGREDIENTS

4 cups cold cooked rice
½ lb uncooked chicken breast, shredded
½ cup cooked ham, shredded
½ cup lean pork, shredded
½ cup canned abalone, shredded
½ cup water chestnuts, sliced
½ cup bamboo shoots, shredded
2 Tbs cold water to loosen the rice
1 cup chicken broth

CONDIMENTS

Mix Sauce
{
2 Tbs soy sauce
1 Tbs sherry
1 tsp salt
⅛ tsp MSG
⅛ tsp pepper
}

2 Tbs peanut oil for frying
1 scallion or ½ dry onion, diced

METHOD

1. Add 2 Tbs cold water to rice and loosen the grains as much as possible.
2. Heat skillet; add oil and heat thoroughly.
3. Fry scallion and pork for 5 minutes. Add chicken and ham and quick fry for 2 minutes.
4. Add sauce. Cook for 1 minute. Add rice and mix well.
5. Add chicken stock and bring to a boil. Lower heat, and add water chestnuts, abalone, and bamboo shoots.
6. Cover pan and simmer for ½ hour.

CHAPTER 14

Noodle Dishes

THE only people on earth who are as fascinated with noodles as the Chinese are the Italians. It was Marco Polo who introduced noodles, spaghetti, ravioli, and even pizza to Italy after his return from the court of Kublai Khan.

Noodles are popular all over China and in the Asiatic countries which were influenced by Chinese culture. In the south of China where rice is the staple food, noodles are eaten as a diversion and are a favorite in-between-meals snack. In the north of China, where the wheat field replaces the rice paddy as the characteristic feature of the landscape, noodles are a staple food at the daily family meals.

Noodles are a symbol of longevity and the dish of noodles is served at birthday celebrations in the manner of the Western birthday cake.

Making noodles is an art which requires great dexterity—the amateur soon finds himself swathed in noodle strings calling for help. Most of the well-to-do families of northern China had a pastry chef who specialized in making noodles, dumplings, steamed breads, and other kinds of pastries.

Chinese noodles are made from various kinds of grains: wheat, rice, and corn, and peas. The pea noodles are also known as transparent noodles and are especially fascinating to our Western friends. They are translucent and have a gelatinous texture. Although they have no flavor of their own they readily absorb the flavors of the other ingredients.

Chinese noodles are made in a variety of shapes and sizes. There are even noodles in the shape of a fish. Most Chinese noodles, however, are on the diminutive side of the noodle scale and there are some varieties which are as fine as silken threads.

Noodles are one staple which can be bought at the Chinese market at a great saving. In the American grocery there are various kinds of egg noodles which are a good substitute for the Chinese noodle.

Noodles should not be washed before they are cooked. They should be stored in a cool dry place.

In Chinese cooking, plain noodles are seldom served and boiling noodles is often a preliminary cooking process. Noodles should be *slowly* added to *boiling* water; the water should be kept at a rolling boil for 6 to 8 minutes or until the noodles are barely tender. Noodles should not be overcooked; they will continue to cook in their own heat after they leave the pan and can become mushy. If the boiling is to be followed by another cooking process such as frying or stewing the noodles should only be 80% done when they are removed from the water. The boiled noodles should be drained in a colander, rinsed with cold water, and separated with a fork. If they are to be served hot they may be kept warm in a double boiler.

Leftover noodles have many uses. They may be used for noodle soup, Chao Mein, or any of the other noodle dishes in this chapter. Chao Mein, in fact, is usually made with leftover noodles since the noodles should be completely cold and dry before they are fried. Leftover spaghetti, without the sauce of course, can be substituted for leftover noodles.

"Chao Mein" means "fried noodles." It is a very popular dish in China as well as in the United States. The American version is quite different from the original Chinese dish, however; in the United States the fried noodles are mass-produced like potato chips and are rather hard and greasy. The recipes in this chapter will be for the authentic Chinese Chao Mein: cold cooked noodles quick-fried with other ingredients in the manner of fried rice.

In general, there are two basic kinds of Chao Mein. In the first type of dish, shredded meats are mixed with eggs before they are cooked with the vegetables and noodles. In the second type of dish, no eggs are used. Various kinds of meats and vegetables may be used to make this dish and there are an infinite number of interesting combinations of ingredients which may be used. The reader should feel free to make any substitutions in the recipes and to use the various oddments in the refrigerator. Chao Mein is a very casual sort of a dish, and can absorb any number of ingredients with good cheer.

CHAO MEIN

INGREDIENTS

pork		
chicken		spinach
ham		green onions
beef	cooked	celery
shrimp	or	cabbage hearts
duck	uncooked	lettuce hearts
game		celery cabbage
eggs		cucumber
		bean sprouts
		bamboo shoots
		mushrooms, dry or fresh
		water chestnuts

Various proportions and combinations of meats and vegetables may be used:

1. An assortment of many different ingredients for Ten Precious Chao Mein: two kinds of meat, one kind of vegetables, mushrooms, and shrimp. The shrimp may be omitted and various combinations of meats may be used: chicken and ham, pork and ham, chicken and pork. Any vegetable may be used.

2. One kind of meat with one kind of vegetable as in Chao Mein with Beef and Spinach.

3. One kind of meat with two kinds of vegetables: use the basic recipe for Chao Mein and make up your own combination of ingredients, such as pork with celery cabbage and bamboo shoots, chicken with bean sprouts and mushrooms etc.

TEN PRECIOUS NOODLES

(CHAO MEIN)

SERVES 4 to 6   METHOD: Hot frying

INGREDIENTS

3 cups cold cooked noodles
½ cup cooked pork, cut in strips
½ cup shrimp, shredded
½ cup cooked ham, cut in strips
2½ cups cabbage, celery, or any vegetable, cut in strips
5 large mushrooms, cut in strips
3 eggs beaten

CONDIMENTS

Mix Sauce
- 2 Tbs soy sauce
- 1 Tbs sherry
- ½ tsp sesame oil
- 1 tsp salt
- pinch of MSG

3 Tbs peanut oil for frying
1 slice of ginger, diced
2 scallions, diced
2 cloves of garlic, minced

METHOD

1. Heat skillet (375°). Add oil and heat thoroughly.
2. Fry scallions, garlic and ginger to a golden brown.
3. Mix meat and shrimp with beaten eggs. Fry in skillet for 2 minutes.
4. Add vegetables and the sauce. Cook for 2 minutes, stirring constantly.
5. Add noodles and mix with all other ingredients. Quick fry for 3 minutes.
6. Serve hot.

CHAO MEIN WITH HAM

SERVES 4 to 6   METHOD: Hot frying

INGREDIENTS

3 cups cold cooked noodles
½ cup cooked ham cut in strips
2 cups celery or celery cabbage
   cut in strips
   or
1 cups of bean sprouts, water
   chestnuts, or bamboo shoots

CONDIMENTS

Mix Sauce { 2 Tbs soy sauce
           ½ tsp salt
           pinch of MSG

3 Tbs peanut oil for frying
2 scallions or ½ dry onion,
   diced
1 clove of garlic, crushed
1 small slice ginger, diced

METHOD

1. Heat skillet (375°). Add oil and heat thoroughly.
2. Fry scallions, garlic and ginger to a golden brown.
3. Add ham and vegetables and cook for 2 minutes stirring constantly.
4. Add sauce and mix thoroughly. Add noodles and mix in with other ingredients. Quick fry for 4 minutes.
5. Serve hot.

CHAO MEIN WITH BEEF AND SPINACH

SERVES 4 to 6   METHOD: Hot-frying

INGREDIENTS

3 cups cold cooked noodles
1 lb tender beef, cooked or uncooked and sliced paper thin in
   ½-inch shreds
1 lb spinach cut in 1½-inch shreds

CONDIMENTS

{ 2 Tbs soy sauce
  1 Tbs sherry
  ½ tsp salt
  pinch of pepper

3 Tbs oil for frying
2 scallions, or ½ dry onion,
   diced
1 clove garlic, crushed
1 very small slice of ginger,
   diced

METHOD

1. Heat skillet (375°). Add oil and heat thoroughly.
2. Fry scallions, garlic, and ginger to a golden brown.
3. Add beef. Cook for 2 minutes, stirring constantly. Add sauce and mix thoroughly. Cook for 2 minutes.
4. Add spinach and cook for 2 minutes, stirring constantly.
5. Add noodles and mix thoroughly with other ingredients. Quick fry for 3 minutes stirring constantly.
6. Serve hot.

CHAO MEIN WITH PORK AND SNOW PEAS

SERVES 4 to 6   METHOD: Hot-frying

INGREDIENTS   ### CONDIMENTS

1 lb cold cooked noodles
½ lb cooked pork cut in strips
1 cup snow peas

Mix Sauce
{
2 Tbs soy sauce
½ tsp salt
pinch of MSG
}

3 tsp peanut oil for frying
2 scallions cut in strips
1 clove of garlic, crushed
1 small slice of ginger

METHOD

1. Heat skillet (375°). Add oil and heat thoroughly.
2. Quick fry cooked pork for 2 minutes. Add noodles and sauce and mix thoroughly. Quick fry for 4 minutes.

3. Add snow peas and cook for 2 minutes.

Uncooked pork may be used but it should be thoroughly cooked before the noodles are added.

NOODLES WITH SAVORY MEAT SAUCE

SERVES 4 to 6

METHOD: Hot frying and simmering

INGREDIENTS

1 cup minced pork or beef (cooked or uncooked)
1 cup vegetables diced
3 cups hot cooked noodles

1½ Tbs cornstarch ⎱ For
2 Tbs water   ⎰ Thickening

CONDIMENTS

Mix Sauce
⎰ 2 Tbs soy sauce
⎪ 1 Tbs sherry
⎪ ½ Tbs brown sugar
⎪ ½ cup tomato sauce
⎪ 1 can chicken or beef
⎱   broth

2 Tbs peanut oil for frying
2 diced scallions or
    ½ dry onion
1 clove of garlic, crushed

METHOD

1. Heat skillet (375°). Add oil and heat thoroughly.
2. Fry scallions and garlic to a light golden.
3. Add meat and vegetables and cook for 12 minutes, stirring constantly.
4. Add sauce and cook for 5 minutes, stirring constantly.
5. Add thickening and stir until smooth.
6. Serve over hot noodles.

CHINESE SPAGHETTI

SERVES 4 to 6   METHOD: Hot frying

INGREDIENTS   CONDIMENTS

1 lb uncooked beef, chicken, or   ⎧ 2 Tbs soy sauce
  ham cut in strips   Mix   ⎪ 1 Tbs sherry
1 cup bean sprouts   Sauce ⎨ ½ tsp salt
1 cup of celery cabbage cut in   ⎩ pinch of MSG
  1-inch strips (any vegetable
  may be used)   1 Tbs peanut oil for frying
6 cups hot cooked noodles

METHOD

1. Heat skillet (350°). Add oil and heat thoroughly.
2. Fry meat until done—3 minutes for beef or chicken breast, 12 minutes for pork or uncooked ham. (If precooked meat is used, brown slightly.)
3. Add sauce and vegetables and cook for 4 minutes, stirring constantly.
4. Serve meat and vegetables on top of hot cooked noodles. They should be kept in separate layers.

HUI MEIN

SERVES 4 to 6   METHOD: Hot frying and stewing

INGREDIENTS   CONDIMENTS

¼ lb uncooked ham cut in strips   ⎧ 2 Tbs soy sauce
¼ lb uncooked shrimp, cut   Mix   ⎪ pinch of MSG
  in strips   Sauce ⎨ pinch of pepper
¼ lb uncooked pork, cut   ⎩ 2 cups chicken or beef broth
  in strips
1½ cups cooked noodles   2 Tbs peanut oil for frying
                                               2 scallions or
                                                 ½ dry onion diced
                                               1 clove of garlic, crushed
                                               1 slice of ginger, diced

METHOD

1. Heat skillet (375°). Add oil and heat thoroughly.
2. Fry scallions, garlic and ginger to a golden brown.
3. Add pork and ham and cook for 8 minutes. Add shrimp and cook for three minutes more, stirring constantly.
4. Add cooked noodles and meat sauce. Cover pan and lower heat.
5. Simmer for 10 minutes.

CHAPTER 15

Salads

EVERYONE loves a good salad, and the Chinese are no exception. Chinese salads are delightful. The vegetables are crisp, well-chilled and brightly colored and the dressing is delicious but not overpowering. For hygienic reasons the Chinese quickly blanched most of their vegetables before they were mixed with the sauce and chilled. This quick scalding brightened the colors of the vegetables and enhanced their taste without destroying their fresh textures. Sesame oil (which is too expensive for most everyday cooking) is used in Chinese salad dressings because of its delightful flavor and fragrance. If you are unable to find sesame oil, any pure vegetable oil may be substituted.

Salads made with cooked meat, poultry, or sea food are especially delicious. This is an excellent way to use leftover pork, roast beef, or chicken.

In making Chinese salads follow the usual rules of salad making. Wash the greens well, toss them lightly in the sauce, and chill them in the refrigerator. Do not let the vegetables sit in the dressing for any length of time if you value the texture of the salad.

Our chapter on vegetables gives instructions for parboiling. Be sure to rinse the greens with cold water immediately after they are removed from the boiling water in order to preserve the texture and color.

SWEET-SOUR CELERY SALAD

SERVES 4 to 6

INGREDIENTS

1 lb celery, cut in thin strips,
    1 to 1½-inch lengths

CONDIMENTS

Salad Dressing
- 2 Tbs soy sauce
- 1 Tbs vinegar
- 1 tsp sesame oil
- 1 tsp sherry
- 1 tsp sugar
- ⅛ tsp MSG

METHOD

1. Parboil celery in boiling water for 2 minutes. Rinse with cold water.
2. Drain and cool for 5 minutes.
3. Add sauce. Chill for 20 minutes in the refrigerator.
4. Serve cold.

TOMATO AND ONION SALAD

SERVES 4 to 6

INGREDIENTS

1 lb tomatoes, sliced thin
2 medium onions, sliced thin

CONDIMENTS

Salad Dressing
- 2 Tbs soy sauce
- ½ Tbs vinegar
- 1 tsp sesame oil
- 1 tsp sugar
- ⅛ tsp MSG

METHOD

1. Seed tomatoes.
2. Mix tomatoes and onions.
3. Add sauce. Chill for 20 minutes in the refrigerator.
4. Serve cold.

BEAN SPROUT SALAD

SERVES 4 to 6

INGREDIENTS   **CONDIMENTS**

1 lb bean sprouts

Salad Dressing
- 2 Tbs soy sauce
- 1 tsp sesame oil
- 1 tsp sugar
- ⅛ tsp MSG

METHOD

1. Pour boiling water over bean sprouts. Rinse with cold water.
2. Drain and cool for 5 minutes.
3. Add sauce. Chill for 20 minutes in the refrigerator.
4. Serve cold.

CUCUMBER SALAD

SERVES 4 to 6

INGREDIENTS   **CONDIMENTS**

1 lb cucumber

Salad Dressing
- 1 Tbs soy sauce
- 1 tsp sherry
- 1 tsp sesame oil
- 1 tsp vinegar
- 1 tsp sugar
- ⅛ tsp MSG

METHOD

1. Peel and halve cucumber. Seed and cut in thin slices.
2. Add dressing. Chill for 20 minutes in the refrigerator.
3. Serve cold.

SPINACH SALAD

SERVES 4 to 6

INGREDIENTS

1 lb spinach cut in thin strips,
   1 to 1½ inches in length

CONDIMENTS

Salad Dressing
- 2 Tbs soy sauce
- 1 Tbs vinegar
- 1 tsp sugar
- ⅛ tsp MSG
- 1 tsp sesame oil
- 1 tsp peanut butter softened in 1 tsp sesame oil

METHOD

1. Parboil spinach for 2 minutes. Rinse in cold water and drain.
2. Add dressing. Chill for 20 minutes in the refrigerator.
3. Serve cold.

ASPARAGUS SALAD

SERVES 4 to 6

INGREDIENTS

1 lb asparagus, cut in pieces,
   1 to 1½ inches in length

CONDIMENTS

Salad Dressing
- 2 Tbs soy sauce
- ½ Tbs vinegar
- 1 tsp sesame oil
- 1 tsp sugar
- ⅛ tsp MSG

METHOD

1. Parboil asparagus in boiling water for 3 minutes. Rinse with cold water.
2. Drain and cool for 5 minutes.
3. Add dressing. Chill for 20 minutes in the refrigerator.
4. Serve cold.

CHICKEN AND BEAN SPROUT SALAD

SERVES 4 to 6

INGREDIENTS

1 lb bean sprouts
¼ lb cooked chicken, cut in strips

CONDIMENTS

Salad Dressing
{
2 Tbs soy sauce
1 tsp sesame oil
⅛ tsp MSG
}

METHOD

1. Pour boiling water over beansprouts. Rinse with cold water.
2. Drain and cool for 5 minutes. Add chicken.
3. Add dressing. Chill for 20 minutes in the refrigerator.
4. Serve cold.

CRABMEAT AND CUCUMBER SALAD

SERVES 4 to 6

INGREDIENTS

1 lb cucumber
½ lb crabmeat

CONDIMENTS

Salad Dressing
{
2 Tbs soy sauce
1 Tbs vinegar
1 tsp sesame oil
⅛ tsp MSG
}

METHOD

1. Peel cucumber, cut in half. Remove seeds and cut into thin slices.
2. Mix crabmeat and cucumber.
3. Add dressing. Chill for 20 minutes in the refrigerator.
4. Serve cold.

CRAB AND ASPARAGUS SALAD

SERVES 4 to 6

INGREDIENTS

1 lb asparagus cut in 1-inch lengths
¼ lb crabmeat

CONDIMENTS

Salad Dressing
{
1 Tbs soy sauce
1 tsp sesame oil
⅛ tsp MSG
}

METHOD

1. Parboil asparagus for 3 minutes. Rinse in cold water and drain.
2. Mix crab and asparagus.
3. Add dressing. Chill for 20 minutes in the refrigerator.
4. Serve cold.

BEEF, TOMATOES AND ONION SALAD

SERVES 4 to 6

INGREDIENTS

½ lb tomatoes, sliced thin
1 onion, sliced thin
½ cup cold roast beef, stripped

CONDIMENTS

Salad Dressing
{ ½ Tbs soy sauce
1 tsp sesame oil
⅛ tsp MSG

METHOD

1. Mix tomatoes, onion, and beef.
2. Add dressing. Chill for 20 minutes in the refrigerator.
3. Serve cold.

CHICKEN AND ASPARAGUS SALAD

SERVES 4 to 6

INGREDIENTS

1 lb asparagus, cut in 1-inch
   lengths
⅔ cup cooked chicken, sliced thin

CONDIMENTS

Salad Dressing
{ 1 Tbs soy sauce
1 tsp sesame oil
⅛ tsp MSG

METHOD

1. Parboil asparagus for 3 minutes. Rinse in cold water. Drain.
2. Mix asparagus and chicken.
3. Add dressing. Chill in the refrigerator for 20 minutes.
4. Serve cold.

ABALONE AND CUCUMBER SALAD

SERVES 4 to 6

INGREDIENTS

1 lb cucumber
½ cup canned abalone,
  sliced very thin in strips

CONDIMENTS

Salad Dressing
{ 1 Tbs soy sauce
  1 tsp sesame oil
  ⅛ tsp MSG

METHOD

1. Peel, cut in half, and slice cucumber thinly.
2. Add abalone.
3. Add dressing. Chill for 20 minutes in the refrigerator.
4. Serve cold.

SHRIMP AND CAULIFLOWER SALAD

SERVES 4 to 6

INGREDIENTS

1 lb cauliflower, shredded
¼ lb cooked shrimp, shredded

CONDIMENTS

Salad Dressing
{ 1 Tbs soy sauce
  1 tsp sesame oil
  ⅛ tsp MSG

METHOD

1. Parboil cauliflower 2 minutes. Rinse in cold water. Drain and dry.
2. Add shrimp. Mix well.
3. Add dressing. Chill for 20 minutes in the refrigerator.
4. Serve cold.

BEEF AND SPINACH SALAD

SERVES 4 to 6

INGREDIENTS

1 lb spinach
⅔ cup cold beef, cut in strips

CONDIMENTS

Salad Dressing
{ 1 Tbs soy sauce
  1 tsp sesame oil
  ⅛ tsp MSG

METHOD

1. Parboil spinach for 2 minutes. Rinse in cold water. Drain and dry.
2. Mix spinach and beef.
3. Add dressing. Chill for 20 minutes in the refrigerator.
4. Serve cold.

HAM AND BEAN SPROUT SALAD

SERVES 4 to 6

INGREDIENTS

1 lb bean sprouts
¾ cup ham, cut in strips

CONDIMENTS

Salad Dressing
- 2 Tbs soy sauce
- 1 Tbs vinegar
- 1 tsp sesame oil
- 1 tsp sugar
- ⅛ tsp MSG

METHOD

1. Pour boiling water over bean sprouts. Rinse in cold water. Drain.
2. Add ham. Mix well.
3. Add dressing. Chill for 20 minutes in the refrigerator.
4. Serve cold.

CHAPTER 16

Vegetables with Vegetable Preparation Charts

"THOU shalt not kill" is the primary tenet of Buddhism and according to this teaching every walking, creeping and swimming thing is sancrosanct. Vegetables are the only thing which a good Buddhist will eat and for centuries, some of the best vegetable cooking has been done in Buddhist monastaries. Buddhism provided an incentive for an art of vegetable cookery which has never been surpassed. Perhaps it is only in a society where many people abstain from meat, that the inherent nobility of the vegetable can be revealed. In the West, vegetables have always been eclipsed by the status of meat, and have never found their rightful place.

When Buddhism first came over the Himalayas, it was rejected by the Chinese as a weird Indian philosophy. It seemed impractical and thoroughly un-Chinese. After many centuries, however, Chinese scholars incorporated Buddhism into Taoism and it became widely accepted in its Chinese form—Chan or Zen as it was known in Japan. The conquests of the Mongols had made the Chinese feel a need for a philosophy which would deal effectively with human suffering.

The religious vegetarianism of Buddhism was grafted onto the scientific study of vegetables which was a part of Taoism, and the result was a vegetable diet which satisfied all human nutritional needs, and was also delicious, varied and interesting.

In the feasts which are held in the Buddhist monastaries, everything from the sharks' fins to the meat balls is composed of vegetables. The vegetable dishes bear an amazing resemblance to their fleshly counterparts in texture and form as well as in taste. The sweet-sour fish, for example, is made of mashed potatoes encased in a fried bean skin in the shape of a fish. The bones are made of celery threads, the eyes of pearls. It is served with the traditional sweet-sour sauce. On ceremonial occasions and funeral exercizes, it is customary to go the monastary for the vegetarian feast.

WASHING AND STORING VEGETABLES

The Chinese do not believe in washing vegetables until they are cooked since they feel that washing the vegetables before they are put in the refrigerator takes the life out of them. Modern scientists have discovered that many water soluble vitamins are lost when vegetables are exposed to water or moisture, for any length of time. It is possible to wash them beforehand, however, *if* they are dried thoroughly with a towel or in a French salad basket immediately after they are immersed in water. Whichever practice you follow, it is essential that the vegetables are not left at room temperature for any length of time, are completely dry before they are put in the refrigerator and are not cut until they are ready to use. Remember that light, air, water, and heat are the enemies of vitamins. Since vitamin C is lost rapidly upon exposure to air, the peels and outer leaves should not be removed before the vegetables and fruits are stored: they should not be cut until they are ready to use since exposed surfaces are especially vulnerable. The produce should be stored in a porcelain or glass hydrater with a tight cover and should be placed on a rack over one-eighth inch of water. Outer leaves and stalks can be used in cooking if they are in good condition.

PREPARATION

Different kinds of vegetables require different kinds of preparation before they are cooked. We can classify vegetables in the following manner:

Group I. These vegetables are fibrous and can be tough if under-
cooked and mushy if overcooked. These vegetables must
be parboiled before they are quick fried.

string beans	broccoli	carrots
asparagus	cauliflower	snow peas

Group II: Softer than Group I, but they have objectionable odors
if they are not scalded with boiling water.

celery	cabbage	bean sprouts

Group III: The following vegetables are tender enough to require
no parboiling.

mushrooms	green pepper	lettuce
spinach	bamboo shoots	tomatoes
celery cabbage	green peas	

Group IV: These vegetables do not require washing after they are
peeled.

eggplant	cucumber	squash

VEGETABLE PREPARATION

GROUP I

Vegetable	Preliminary Treatment	Cutting
ASPARAGUS	Parboil for 2-3 minutes. Put in colander. Rinse in cold water and drain. If tough stalks are used, parboil 1 minute longer before using in hot frying (Chao) dishes.	Cut on the diagonal in pieces 1½ inches long
BROCCOLI	Same as above	Cut in small irregular pieces
CAULIFLOWER	Same as above	Same as above

CARROTS	Same as above	Cut on the diagonal. If the carrots are large, cut in long strips before diagonal cutting.
STRING BEANS	Same as above	Cut on the diagonal in pieces 1½ inches long
SNOW PEAS (bean pods)	Same as above	Use whole

CHART ON VEGETABLE PREPARATIONS

GROUP II

Name	Preliminary Treatment	Cutting
CABBAGE*	Put in colander. Scald with boiling water. Rinse with cold water and drain.	Shred coarsely or cut in 1-inch lengths
CELERY*	Same as above	Cut on the diagonal to match other ingredients. For small pieces, cut in long strips and then slice
BEAN SPROUTS	Same as above	Do not cut

VEGETABLE PREPARATION CHART

GROUP III

Name	Preliminary Treatment	Cutting
BAMBOO SHOOTS	No preliminary cooking required. Just wash.	Cut to match other ingredients. Remove calcium deposits at the center

* Celery and cabbage may also be diced or shredded in certain recipes.

CELERY CABBAGE	Same as above	Straight-cut in 1½-inch pieces
GREEN PEPPER	Same as above	Cut to match other ingredients
GREEN PEAS	Same as above	
LETTUCE	Same as above	Shred coarsely, dice or mince
MUSHROOMS	Wash thoroughly. Soak dried mushrooms	Cut to match other ingredients
SPINACH	Wash thoroughly	Cut in 1½-inch lengths. May be diced or minced in certain recipes
TOMATOES	Wash thoroughly	Cut to harmonize with other ingredients. Cut in slices or segments

VEGETABLE PREPARATION CHART

GROUP IV

Name	*Preliminary Treatment*	*Cutting*
CUCUMBER	Peel, do not wash	Halve, seed, cut in thin slices straight across
EGGPLANT	Same as above	Cut in 1-inch cubes
SUMMER SQUASH	Same as above	Cut in ¼-inch slices
ZUCCINI	Same as above	Cut in ¼-inch slices

NOTE ON SNOW PEAS

Snow peas are also known as "sugar peas" or "Chinese peas." They are eaten in the pod; unlike garden-variety peas, the pods of snow peas are tender and unstringy. Snow peas are a Cantonese vegetable and were not widely available in China because of transportation difficulties and the absence of refrigeration. They were brought to the United States by the Cantonese and became very popular.

Snow peas are especially appropriate in Cantonese dishes such as Sub Gum, and Ten Precious Chao Mein. They go well with any type of Chop Suey and may be substituted for other vegetables. Since they are long in shape, they harmonize with dishes in which the ingredients are cut in strips; they would go with any type of chao mein but would not harmonize with fried rice.

Because they are valued for their texture, snow peas are used in quick-fried dishes. They are not appropriate in *Hung Shao* dishes or in any dish which requires long cooking or roasting.

The following recipes all use the Chao *or* Hot-Fry *Method.* The pan should be hot before the oil is added, and the oil hot before the vegetables are added. The hot oil seals in the juices of the vegetables and preserves the vitamin C content. (Vitamin C is lost rapidly upon exposure to air.) The vegetables are cut in small pieces for rapid cooking. They should be stirred constantly while they are cooking.

The sauce enhances the flavor of the vegetables. It should be mixed before the vegetables are cooked. The cornstarch should be mixed with the stock or water a few minutes before it is to be used. It should be mixed to a smooth paste and must be constantly stirred after it has been added to the pan or it will become lumpy.

Be sure to follow instruction on the preparation chart before beginning any of these vegetable recipes.

PEAS WITH MUSHROOMS

SERVES 4 to 6   METHOD: Hot frying

INGREDIENTS   **CONDIMENTS**

2 pkg frozen peas
1 cup fresh mushrooms, cut in
   half if large

Mix Sauce
{
2 Tbs soy sauce
1 tsp sugar
⅛ tsp MSG
}

½ cup chicken broth ⎱ Mix
1 tsp cornstarch   ⎰ Thickening

3 Tbs peanut oil for frying
1 scallion or ½ medium
   sized dry onion, diced

METHOD

1. Heat skillet (350°). Add oil and heat thoroughly.
2. Fry scallion until golden brown.
3. Add mushrooms and quick fry for 3 minutes.
4. Add peas and quick fry for 4 minutes.
5. Add sauce and thickening and quick fry for 2 minutes.

CELERY CABBAGE

SERVES 4 to 6   METHOD: Hot frying

INGREDIENTS   **CONDIMENTS**

1 lb celery cabbage, cut in
   1½-inch pieces

See Condiments, Peas with Mushrooms, above

½ cup chicken broth ⎱ Mix
1 tsp cornstarch   ⎰ Thickening

METHOD

Follow Steps 1 and 2, Peas with Mushrooms, above.
3. Add celery cabbage and quick fry for 3 minutes.
4. Add sauce and thickening and quick fry for 2 minutes.

ASPARAGUS

SERVES 4 to 6

METHOD: Hot frying

INGREDIENTS

1 lb asparagus cut on diagonal into 1½-inch pieces

½ cup chicken broth ⎱ Mix
1 tsp cornstarch ⎰ Thickening

CONDIMENTS

See Condiments, Peas with Mushrooms, page 201

METHOD

Follow Steps 1 and 2, Peas with Mushrooms, page 201.
3. Add asparagus and quick fry for 3 minutes.
4. Add sauce and thickening and quick fry for 1 minute.

GREEN BEANS

SERVES 4 to 6

METHOD: Hot frying

INGREDIENTS

1 lb green beans or 2 pkgs frozen beans

½ cup chicken broth ⎱ Mix
1 tsp cornstarch ⎰ Thickening

CONDIMENTS

See Condiments, Peas with Mushrooms, page 201

METHOD

Follow Steps 1 and 2, Peas with Mushrooms, page 201.
3. Add green beans and quick fry for 2 minutes.
4. Add sauce and thickening and quick fry for 2 minutes.

ZUCCINI

SERVES 4 to 6

METHOD: Hot frying

INGREDIENTS

CONDIMENTS

1 lb peeled zuccini,
  cut in 1½-inch pieces

See Condiments, Peas with Mushrooms, page 201

½ cup chicken broth ⎱ Mix
1 tsp cornstarch   ⎰ Thickening

METHOD

Follow Steps 1 and 2, Peas with Mushrooms, page 201.
3. Add zuccini and quick fry for 4 minutes.
4. Add sauce and thickening and quick fry for 1 minute.

BOK CHOY*
(PAI TSAI)

SERVES 4 to 6

METHOD: Hot frying

INGREDIENTS

CONDIMENTS

1 lb bok choy, cut straight
  in 2-inch pieces

Mix ⎧ 1 Tbs soy sauce
Sauce ⎨ ½ tsp sugar
     ⎩ ⅛ tsp MSG

½ cup chicken broth ⎱ Mix
1 tsp cornstarch   ⎰ Thickening

3 Tbs peanut oil for frying
1 scallion or ½ medium
  dry onion stripped

METHOD

Follow Steps 1 and 2, Peas with Mushrooms, page 201.
3. Add bok choy. Quick fry for 3 minutes.
4. Add sauce and thickening and quick fry for 1 minute.

* A special Chinese vegetable which may be available only in certain regions of
the country.

SPINACH

SERVES 4 to 6   METHOD: Hot frying

INGREDIENTS   **CONDIMENTS**

1 lb fresh spinach or   *See* Condiments, Peas with Mush-
  2 pkgs frozen spinach   rooms, page 201

½ cup chicken broth ⎤ Mix
1 tsp cornstarch   ⎦ Thickening

METHOD

Follow Steps 1 and 2, Peas with Mushrooms, page 201.
3. Add spinach and quick fry for 4 minutes.
4. Add sauce and thickening and quick fry for 1 minute.

SUMMER SQUASH

SERVES 4 to 6   METHOD: Hot frying

INGREDIENTS   **CONDIMENTS**

1 lb squash, peeled and   Mix ⎧ 2 Tbs soy sauce
  sliced ¼-inch thick   Sauce ⎨ 1 tsp sugar
                                       ⎩ ⅛ tsp MSG

½ cup chicken broth ⎤ Mix
1 tsp cornstarch   ⎦ Thickening   3 Tbs peanut oil for frying
                                       1 scallion or 1 medium-
                                         sized onion diced
                                       1 clove garlic, minced

METHOD

Follow Steps 1 and 2, Peas with Mushrooms, page 201.
3. Add squash and quick fry for 6 or 7 minutes. Stir constantly.
4. Add garlic, cook 1 minute.
5. Add sauce and thickening and quick fry for 2 minutes.

BROCCOLI

SERVES 4 to 6   METHOD: Hot frying

INGREDIENTS

1 lb broccoli, cut in small
    irregular pieces, or 2 pkg
    frozen broccoli

½ cup chicken broth ⎱ Mix
1 tsp cornstarch   ⎰ Thickening

CONDIMENTS

See Condiments, Peas with Mushrooms, page 201

METHOD

Follow Steps 1 and 2, Peas with Mushrooms, page 201.
3. Add broccoli and quick fry for 3 minutes.
4. Add sauce and thickening and quick fry for 1 minute.

CAULIFLOWER

SERVES 4 to 6   METHOD: Hot frying

INGREDIENTS

1 lb cauliflower, broken into
    small pieces or flowers

½ cup chicken broth ⎱ Mix
1 tsp cornstarch   ⎰ Thickening

CONDIMENTS

Mix   ⎧ 1½ Tbs soy sauce
Sauce ⎨ 1 tsp sugar
      ⎩ ⅛ tsp MSG

3 Tbs peanut oil for frying
1 scallion or ½ medium-
    sized dry onion, diced

METHOD

Follow Steps 1 and 2, Peas with Mushrooms, page 201.
3. Add cauliflower and quick fry for 4 minutes.
4. Add sauce and thickening and quick fry for 1 minute.

PEAS

SERVES 4 to 6   METHOD: Hot frying

INGREDIENTS

1 lb fresh peas or
2 pkg frozen peas

½ cup chicken broth ⎤ Mix
1 tsp cornstarch   ⎦ Thickening

CONDIMENTS

Mix ⎧ 1 Tbs soy sauce
Sauce ⎨ 1 tsp sugar
      ⎩ ⅛ tsp MSG

3 Tbs peanut oil for frying
1 scallion or ½ medium
   dry onion diced

METHOD

Follow Steps 1 and 2, Peas with Mushrooms, page 201.
3. Add peas and quick fry for 3 minutes.
4. Add sauce and thickening and quick fry for 1 minute.

BEAN SPROUTS AND CELERY

SERVES 4 to 6   METHOD: Hot frying

INGREDIENTS

1 lb beansprouts
1 stalk celery, sliced on the
   diagonal in 1-inch strips

½ cup chicken broth ⎤ Mix
1 tsp cornstarch   ⎦ Thickening

CONDIMENTS

Mix ⎧ 2 Tbs soy sauce
Sauce ⎨ 1 tsp sugar
      ⎪ 1 tsp salt
      ⎩ ½ tsp MSG

3 Tbs peanut oil for frying
1 scallion, cut in strips
1 small piece ginger, minced

METHOD

Follow Steps 1 and 2, Peas with Mushrooms, page 201.
3. Add vegetables and quick fry for 2 minutes.
4. Add sauce and thickening and quick fry for 2 minutes.

EGGPLANT

SERVES 4 to 6   METHOD: Hot frying

INGREDIENTS   **CONDIMENTS**

1 medium eggplant, peeled
and cut in 1½-inch pieces

Mix Sauce { 2 Tbs soy sauce
1 tsp sugar
⅛ tsp MSG

½ cup chicken broth } Mix
1 tsp cornstarch — Thickening

5 Tbs peanut oil for frying
2 cloves of garlic,
minced fine
1 large onion, diced

METHOD

Follow Steps 1 and 2, Peas with Mushrooms, page 201.
3. Add eggplant and cook for 5 minutes, stirring constantly.
4. Add two cloves of garlic, minced fine.
5. Add sauce and thickening and quick fry for 3 minutes, stirring constantly.

SWEET AND SOUR ASPARAGUS

SERVES 4 to 6   METHOD: Hot frying

INGREDIENTS   **CONDIMENTS**

1 lb asparagus, cut in
diagonally 1½-inch pieces

1 Tbs cornstarch } Mix
2 Tbs water — Thickening

Mix Sauce { 1 Tbs soy sauce
1 Tbs sherry
4 Tbs vinegar
4 Tbs sugar
1 tsp salt
⅛ tsp MSG
pepper to taste

2 Tbs peanut oil for frying

METHOD

1. Heat skillet (375°). Add oil, heat thoroughly.
2. Add asparagus and quick fry for 4 minutes.
3. Add sauce and quick fry for 2 minutes.
4. Add thickening and quick fry for 1 minute.

SWEET AND SOUR ZUCCINI

SERVES 4 to 6   METHOD: Hot frying

INGREDIENTS   ### CONDIMENTS

1 lb zuccini, peeled and   ⎧ 1 Tbs soy sauce
  cut in 1-inch pieces   │ 4 Tbs vinegar
     Mix   ⎨ 4 Tbs sugar
     Sauce   │ 1 tsp salt
1 Tbs cornstarch ⎱ Mix   ⎩ ⅛ tsp MSG
2 Tbs water   ⎰ Thickening

2 Tbs peanut oil for frying

METHOD

1. Heat skillet (375°). Add oil, heat thoroughly.
2. Add zuccini and quick fry for 4 minutes.
3. Add sauce and quick fry for 2 minutes.
4. Add thickening and quick fry for 1 minute.

SWEET AND SOUR RED CABBAGE

SERVES 4 to 6   METHOD: Hot frying

INGREDIENTS   ### CONDIMENTS

1 lb cabbage, shredded   ⎧ 1 Tbs soy sauce
     Mix   │ 4 Tbs sugar
     Sauce   ⎨ 3 Tbs vinegar
1 Tbs cornstarch ⎱ Mix   ⎩ 1 tsp salt
2 Tbs water   ⎰ Thickening

one or two drops of Tabasco
sauce
2 Tbs peanut oil for frying

METHOD

1. Heat skillet (375°). Add oil, heat thoroughly.
2. Add red cabbage and quick fry for 4 minutes.
3. Add sauce and quick fry for 2 minutes.
4. Add thickening and quick fry for 1 minute.

SWEET AND SOUR CELERY

SERVES 4 to 6   METHOD: Hot frying

INGREDIENTS

1 lb celery, shredded

1 Tbs cornstarch ⎫ Mix
2 Tbs water   ⎰ Thickening

CONDIMENTS

Mix ⎰ 1 Tbs soy sauce
Sauce ⎱ 4 Tbs sugar
     3 Tbs vinegar
     ½ tsp salt

one or two drops of
Tabasco sauce
2 Tbs peanut oil for frying

METHOD

1. Heat skillet (375°). Add oil, heat thoroughly.
2. Add celery and quick fry for 4 minutes.
3. Add sauce and quick fry for 2 minutes.
4. Add thickening and quick fry for 1 minute.

CHAPTER 17

In China, soup had a very important place on the table. Since the Chinese do not drink water, the soup bowl had the same role as the Western water goblet. Between courses, and especially after dry or salty dishes, light and delicious soups were served.

THE PRIMARY STOCK

The flavor of soup depends on the quality of the primary stock. The quality which Chinese gourmets admire in soup is "purity"; this means that the stock must be rich, concentrated, and strained of all residue. Such stock requires a great deal of meat and relatively little liquid and cannot be considered an economy. Many readers will feel that it is not worthwhile to boil down a large quantity of meat for a quart of stock when there is such an agreeable substitute on the American market: Canned chicken and turkey broth. These clear soups are concentrated, flavorful, economical, and are free of residue and impurities. They may be used as a base for any number of interesting soups. The canned soups are great time-savers; it is possible to cook in minutes a soup that formerly required hours of time.

LEFTOVERS

In Chinese cookery, everything is utilized, and many of the leftovers go into the soup. Leftover chicken, beef, and pork bones may be used to enrich the clear canned stock. When the better part of a chicken breast has been stripped away for a quick-fry dish, the remainder goes into the soup pot. Chicken and ham harmonize in many of the rich and expensive Chinese clear soups so it is a good idea to save a bit of the Sunday ham for the pot.

Many kinds of vegetables may be added to the chicken stock alone or in combination: green peas, turnips cut in strips, celery, cabbage, spinach, onions, carrots. Cooked rice or leftover noodles may also be added.

Rules for Soup

1. Vegetables in soup are no exception to the general rule for vegetables: they must not be soggy or overcooked. Vegetables should be added to the soup only a short time before it is to be served.
2. Velvet soups should be velvety. Any lumps are a disgrace. The cornstarch should be mixed smoothly with water, the soup must be stirred constantly after the thickening has been added.
3. Clear soups should be clear. If meat is added it should be cooked for a fairly short time. Cooking soup "by the hour" can result in a muddy looking soup unless it is carefully strained.
4. Meat which is served in soup should be flavorful and not overcooked. If every last bit of flavor is to go into the soup, the meat should be removed before serving. If rich soup is desired, the meat should be added to cold stock or water. If the meat is to be served with the soup, it should be added to boiling liquid so that the juices will be sealed in.
5. Watery soup is to be avoided at all cost. A soup is only as good as the ingredients which go into it. Long cooking cannot transform a few bare bones and one or two shreds of meat into a rich, pure soup.

Light Soups

Light clear soups are often served at dinner since they do not detract from the other dishes. Smooth velvety soups, such as Egg Flower Pork Soup have a rich flavor and texture but are really very light. Sour-Pungent Soup is a very fine soup to serve at a dinner party since it has an intriguing flavor and is unusual and distinctive.

HEAVY SOUPS

For family lunches and light dinners a thick, "meal-in-itself" soup is delicious and easy to make. Such soups are often more solid than liquid and any number of ingredients may be used. Leftover rice may be used with other ingredients to make a thick "congee" or semiliquid soup. Noodles may be combined with such things as mushrooms, sliced abalone, celery, and bean sprouts for hearty noodle soup. Just heat some clear canned chicken stock, adding various leftover ingredients which have been cut in strips or shredded.

EGG FLOWER PORK SOUP

SERVES 4 to 6

INGREDIENTS

½ lb lean pork, cut in fine strips
1 scallion or ½ dry onion,
  cut in fine strips
2 eggs, beaten
3 cups canned chicken broth
3 cups water

1 Tbs cornstarch ⎱ Mix
¼ cup water   ⎰ Thickening

CONDIMENTS

2 Tbs soy sauce
1 tsp sherry
⅛ tsp pepper

1 Tbs peanut oil for frying

METHOD

1. Fry scallion to a light golden brown.
2. Add pork and quick fry for 8 minutes.
3. Drain oil from pan. Add chicken broth, water, and condiments and bring to a boil. Remove from heat.
4. Slowly dribble beaten egg into boiling water to form "flowers."
5. Add thickening and stir for 1 minute. Serve immediately.

CHICKEN SOUP

SERVES 4 to 6

INGREDIENTS

1 2 to 3 lb stewing chicken,
  whole
8 cups water

CONDIMENTS

1 Tbs sherry or sauterne
2 Tbs salt
1 thin slice of ginger,
  diced finely, or a dash
  of ginger powder
⅛ tsp MSG
⅛ tsp pepper
1 scallion or ½ dry onion,
  chopped finely

METHOD

1. Bring water to a boil.
2. Add chicken and condiments. Boil in a covered pan for 1½ hours.
3. Lower heat and simmer for ½ hour.
4. Serve soup in bowls. Serve chicken on a platter.

CHICKEN AND CUCUMBER SOUP

SERVES 4 to 6

INGREDIENTS

2 cans chicken stock
2 cups water
½ small cucumber, peeled, cut in
  half, seeded, and slice thin

CONDIMENTS

1½ tsp salt
⅛ tsp MSG

METHOD

1. Add water and condiments to stock and bring to a boil.
2. Add cucumber slices. Serve immediately. The cucumbers should be crisp. There should be approximately 6 half slices of cucumber for each bowl of soup.

CHICKEN SOUP WITH CRAB LEGS

SERVES 4 to 6

INGREDIENTS

2 cans chicken stock
2 cups water
8 to 12 crab legs, cooked

CONDIMENTS

1½ tsp salt
½ tsp soy sauce
⅛ tsp MSG

METHOD

1. Bring stock to a boil. (The stock may be kept hot on the stove without harm.)
2. Add crab legs and serve immediately.

CELERY CABBAGE AND HAM SOUP

SERVES 4 to 6

INGREDIENTS

1 head celery cabbage, cut
  in 1½-inch lengths
¼ lb boned, precooked ham,
  cut in strips
3 cups water
3 cups canned chicken broth

CONDIMENTS

1 Tbs soy sauce
1 Tbs sherry
1 tsp salt
⅛ tsp pepper

METHOD

1. Put ham, condiments, and broth into a soup pan and bring to a boil. Boil 5 minutes.
2. Add celery cabbage and simmer for 10 minutes, tightly covered.

SOUR AND PUNGENT SOUP

SERVES 4 to 6

INGREDIENTS

¼ lb uncooked chicken breast,
   sliced thin in 1-inch strips
¼ lb lean pork, sliced thin in
   1-inch strips
4 cups canned chicken or
   turkey broth
3 cups water

3 Tbs cornstarch ⎤ Mix
4 Tbs water   ⎦ Thickening

CONDIMENTS

Mix
Sauce
⎧ 1 Tbs salt
⎪ 1 Tbs sherry
⎪ 1 scallion cut in strips
⎨ ½ cup white vinegar or
⎪   lemon juice
⎪ 2 tsp pepper
⎪ 1 slice of ginger, diced
⎩ ⅛ tsp MSG

METHOD

1. Bring chicken broth and water to a boil in a deep pan.
2. Add chicken and pork to broth and boil for 20 minutes.
3. Add sauce and mix thoroughly.
4. Add thickening and stir until smooth (about 1 minute).
5. Serve immediately.

VELVET CHICKEN SOUP WITH CORN I

SERVES 4 to 6

INGREDIENTS

3 diced uncooked chicken
   breasts
1 large can creamed corn
   (#2½)
1 slice cooked ham, diced,
   for a garnish
3 cups canned chicken broth
3 cups water

3 Tbs cornstarch ⎤ Mix
½ cup water   ⎦ Thickening

CONDIMENTS

1 Tbs sherry
1 Tbs salt
⅛ tsp MSG

METHOD

1. Add condiments to chicken broth and water. Bring to a boil in a deep pan.
2. Add creamed corn and chicken. Bring to a boil, stirring constantly for 5 minutes.
3. Reduce heat to low.
4. Add thickening and stir constantly for 2 minutes.
5. Serve immediately with the ham as a garnish.

VELVET CHICKEN SOUP WITH CORN II

SERVES 4 to 6

INGREDIENTS	CONDIMENTS
1 large can creamed corn	1 Tbs sherry
3 eggs, beaten	1 Tbs salt
1 slice cooked ham, diced, for a garnish	⅛ tsp MSG
3 cups chicken broth	
3 cups water	

3 Tbs cornstarch ⎱ Mix
½ cup water   ⎰ Thickening

METHOD

1. Add condiments to chicken broth and water in a deep pan. Bring to a boil.
2. Add creamed corn and bring to a boil. Cook for 3 minutes, stirring constantly. Reduce heat to low.
3. Dribble beaten eggs into soup to form "flowers."
4. Add thickening. Cook for 1 minute, stirring constantly.
5. Garnish with ham and serve immediately.

VEGETABLE SOUP

SERVES 4 to 6

INGREDIENTS

¼ lb cabbage, cut in strips
¼ lb carrots, cut in strips
¼ lb celery, cut in strips
1 scallion or ½ dry onion,
   cut in strips
3 cups canned chicken broth
3 cups water

CONDIMENTS

Mix Sauce:
- 2 Tbs soy sauce
- 1 tsp sherry
- 1 tsp salt
- ⅛ tsp pepper
- ⅛ tsp MSG

1 Tbs peanut oil for frying

METHOD

1. Heat soup pan. Add oil and heat thoroughly.
2. Fry vegetables for 1 minute.
3. Drain off excess oil. Add broth and water. Add sauce and simmer for 15 minutes, tightly covered.

FISH BALL SOUP

SERVES 4 to 6

INGREDIENTS

Mix together for fish balls:
- ½ lb white fish, minced
- ¼ cup lean pork, minced
- 2 Tbs cornstarch
- 1 egg, beaten

3 cups canned chicken broth
3 cups water

CONDIMENTS

- 2 Tbs soy sauce
- 1 Tbs sherry
- ½ tsp MSG
- ⅛ tsp pepper
- 1 scallion or ½ dry onion, diced
- 1 thin slice of ginger, diced

METHOD

1. Bring chicken broth and water to a boil in a large pan.
2. Mix all other ingredients and condiments together.
3. Form into small balls ½ inch in diameter.
4. Drop fish balls into boiling broth and cook for 10 minutes in a covered pan.

NOODLE SOUP

SERVES 4 to 6

INGREDIENTS

CONDIMENTS

3 cups chicken broth
3 cups water
2 cups diced cooked chicken
   or any other meat
2 to 4 cups cooked noodles
1 cup leftover vegetables

1 tsp salt
⅛ tsp MSG

METHOD

1. Heat chicken broth, condiments, and water to boiling.
2. Add chicken, cooked noodles, and bring to a boil.
3. Add vegetables. Simmer 3 minutes. Serve.

CHAPTER 18

Sweet Things

Many people in the United States are unfamiliar with the Chinese sweet dishes because they are not usually served in Chinese restaurants here. It is also a surprise for most to find that the Chinese traditionally serve sweet dishes throughout the meal—not at the end. The Chinese like a dash of sweetness between courses as a change of pace, to contrast with the salty and highly seasoned main dishes. Today, because of the influence of Western customs, many Chinese families are adopting the idea of serving sweet dishes at the end of the meal and are using the traditional Chinese sweets as desserts.

The recipes which follow can be made to serve both as the traditional Chinese sweet or as the more customary American end-of-the-meal dessert.

ALMOND TEA I

Serves 4 to 6

1 cup blanched almonds
½ cup raw rice

4 cups cold water
½ cup sugar

METHOD

1. Put rice and almonds through the fine setting of a food mill.
2. Add rice and almonds to water in a pan with sugar.
3. Bring to a boil.
4. Turn down the heat, cover and simmer for 30 minutes.
5. Serve hot in small soup bowls.

ALMOND TEA II

1¼ cup almond paste   ½ cup sugar
4 cups water

METHOD

1. Add almond paste to cold water and mix well with an eggbeater. Add sugar.
2. Bring to a boil and serve hot in small soup bowls.

MANDARIN ORANGE

SERVES 4 to 6

2 small #1½ cans Mandarin   4 cups water
  oranges or tangerines with   ½ cup sugar
  the syrup (or 1 large #2½ can)
                                    Mix   ⌠2 Tbs cornstarch
                                    Thickening   ⌡4 Tbs water

METHOD

1. Boil 2 cups water. Add fruit and sugar.
2. Add remaining 2 cups water and thickening.
3. Stir constantly and bring to the boiling point. Serve hot in soup bowls.

PRECIOUS FRUIT I*

SERVES 4 to 6

1 large can fruit cocktail with the syrup   Mix   ⌠2 Tbs cornstarch
½ cup sugar   Thickening   ⌡2 Tbs water
4 cups water

* Fresh fruit is very good in the Precious Fruit recipes. If fresh fruit is used, about 2 cups of fresh, canned or frozen fruit juice should be used in place of 2 cups of the water.

METHOD

1. Boil 2 cups water. Add fruit and sugar.
2. Add remaining 2 cups water and thickening. Bring to boiling point but do not boil. Stir constantly.
3. Serve hot in soup bowls.

PRECIOUS FRUIT II

SERVES 4 to 6

1 can grapefruit with syrup
1 cup sugar
4 cups water

Mix Thickening { 1½ Tbs cornstarch
1½ Tbs water

METHOD

1. Boil 2 cups water. Add fruit and sugar.
2. Add remaining 2 cups water and thickening.
3. Heat again. Bring to the boiling point but do not boil. Stir constantly.
4. Serve hot in soup bowls.

ALMOND CURD I

SERVES 4 to 6

1 quart of milk
2 pkg unflavored gelatin
½ cup water

½ cup sugar
1 Tbs almond extract

METHOD

1. Soften gelatin in ½ cup water.
2. Scald milk.
3. Add sugar, gelatin, and almond extract to milk.
4. Pour into bowls and refrigerate until firm.
5. Serve plain or topped with slivered almonds.

ALMOND CURD II

SERVES 4 to 6

1 quart milk   ½ cup sugar
2 pkg unflavored gelatin   1 Tbs almond extract
½ cup water   1 can fruit cocktail or tangerines

METHOD

1. Soften gelatin in ½ cup water.
2. Scald milk.
3. Add sugar, gelatin, and almond extract to milk.
4. Pour into bowls. Refrigerate until firm.
5. Add fruit cocktail before serving.

WALNUT DATES

SERVES 4 to 6

1 cup dates, pitted   8 cups water
2 cups walnuts   1 cup sugar
1 cup water   ½ cup uncooked rice

METHOD

1. Mix all ingredients, using 1 cup of water.
2. Put mixture through a food grinder to form a paste.
3. Add remaining 8 cups of water and bring to a boil.
4. Serve hot in bowls.

HONEY BANANA

SERVES 4 to 6

4 bananas, quartered   ⎡ 2 cups of sugar
4 Tbs oil for frying   Syrup ⎨ 1½ cups water
                                           ⎣ ½ Tbs vinegar

METHOD

1. Boil water, sugar, and vinegar, until it forms a hard ball when dropped in cold water.
2. Heat oil in skillet. Fry bananas for 2 minutes.
3. Dip bananas in syrup.

APPLE OR PEAR COMPOTE

SERVES 4 to 6

6 large pears, or apples, peeled and cored   ½ cup chopped dates
6 Tbs honey   ½ cup chopped walnuts

METHOD I

1. Fill cavity of pears or apples with a mixture of chopped dates and walnuts.
2. Coat pears or apples with honey.
3. Put pears or apples on a rack in a steamer. Add ¾-inch water and steam on a moderate heat for 45 minutes or until tender. The time varies with the type of fruit.

METHOD II

(This is a Westernized version of this dessert.)

1. Fill pears or apples with the date-nut mixture as in Method 1.
2. Put pears or apples in a greased casserole. Add

⅓ cup brown sugar   1 cup sauterne

3. Cover casserole and bake in a 325° oven for 45 minutes or until tender.

Note: If apples are used, sprinkle with cinnamon before serving.

TEN PRECIOUS RICE PUDDING

SERVES 4 to 6

2 cups uncooked rice*
1 cup sugar
2 Tbs lard
½ cup raisins

½ cup pitted dates
½ cup boiled, shelled chestnuts
   or walnuts
2 Tbs assorted candied fruits

METHOD

1. Wash rice. Add water to 1 inch above rice. Boil in a covered pan for fifteen minutes.
2. Add sugar, lard, raisins, dates, nuts, and candied fruits.
3. Steam for 45 to 50 minutes. It may also be cooked in the top of a double boiler.

HIDDEN TREASURE RICE PUDDING

SERVES 4 to 6

This is a Westernized version of the Traditional Chinese steamed rice pudding. The people of the West introduced the oven-baking of desserts and the method was enthusiastically adopted by many Chinese cooks.

4 cups cooked rice, loosened with
   ½ cup water
1 cup sugar
2 Tbs soft butter or lard

Mix
   ½ cup raisins
   1 cup chopped pitted dates
   ½ cup chopped walnuts
   2 Tbs candied fruit (optional)

METHOD

1. Add sugar and lard to rice. Mix thoroughly.
2. Grease a casserole. Add rice mixture.

* Glutinous rice is used for desserts in China. It may be bought in Chinese stores and is the best rice for this dish. If unobtainable, use the round sticky rice.

3. Make a cavity in rice mixture. Add fruit-nut mixture. Cover with 2 inches of rice.
4. Cover casserole and bake in a 325° oven for 45 minutes.

PEKING DUST

SERVES 4 to 6

1 lb unshelled chestnuts
1 cup whipped cream
½ cup sugar

1 tsp salt
¼ cup maraschino cherries

METHOD

1. Cook chestnuts in salted water until soft. Cool.
2. Remove shell and skin. Mince finely.
3. Add sugar to minced chestnuts.
4. Top with whipped cream and maraschino cherries.

GREEN PEA CAKE

SERVES 4 to 6

1 cup dried green peas
3 cups water
¼ cup whole maraschino cherries

1 cup sugar
1 pkg unflavored gelatin softened
   in ¼ cup water

METHOD

1. Boil peas covered for 1 hour in 3 cups water.
2. Add sugar and gelatin softened in water.
3. Bring to a boil. Reduce heat and simmer for 3 minutes.
4. Pour into square mold. Refrigerate until solid. Cut in 1-inch squares.
5. Top with a cherry and serve.

ICE CREAM PUFFS

SERVES 4 to 6

1 quart ice cream, vanilla or straw-
  berry
4 eggs, well beaten ⎫
4 level Tbs flour   ⎬ Pastry
½ tsp baking powder ⎭

3 inches peanut oil in a skillet for
  deep frying

METHOD

1. Make 6 ice-cream balls with ice-cream scoop. Put them on wax paper squares and put them in the deep freeze or the freezing compartment of the refrigerator until they are hard.
2. Combine flour, baking powder and beaten eggs. Coat ice-cream balls with this mixture. Return to freezer until very hard.
3. Just before dessert is to be served, heat peanut oil to 365°. Add another coating of pastry mixture.
4. Fry ice-cream balls in deep fat until pastry covering puffs up (only a few seconds). Serve immediately.

ALMOND COOKIES

SERVES 4 to 6

2½ cups flour
1 cup sugar
½ tsp baking soda
1 cup shortening (lard, chicken fat or butter)
2 eggs, beaten

⅛ tsp salt
1 Tbs almond extract
¼ lb whole almonds, blanched

METHOD

1. Mix dry ingredients.
2. Cut shortening into dry ingredients.
3. Add beaten eggs. Stir until well mixed. Add almond extract.

4. Roll out dough. Shape into circles 1½ inches in diameter.
5. Put on a greased baking sheet with an almond in the center of each cookie.
6. Bake in a 325° oven for 25 minutes.

SESAME COOKIES

SERVES 4 to 6

2 cups all-purpose flour
1 cup sugar
1 tsp baking powder
½ cup shortening
2 unbeaten eggs

1 cup sesame seeds

METHOD

1. Sift dry ingredients. Add eggs and shortening. Mix well.
2. Knead dough for 5 to 7 minutes. Add a small amount of water if too dry.
3. Roll in a long piece and cut in circles ⅛-inch thick and 1½ inches in diameter.
4. Top with sesame seeds and bake in a 300° oven for 18 minutes.

CAKE OF GOOD FORTUNE I

SERVES 4 to 6

1½ cups sifted whole wheat or white pastry flour ⎫
1 cup sugar   ⎬ Sift Together
3 Tbs baking powder   ⎭

½ cup butter, lard or peanut oil
2 unbeaten eggs
1 cup evaporated milk

1 cup ground blanched almonds
1 tsp almond flavoring (optional)

METHOD

1. Sift dry ingredients together over shortening.
2. Add eggs and ½ cup milk. Mix until moist.
3. Beat on the slow speed of an electric beater for 1 minute or 100 strokes by hand.
4. Add ½ cup of milk and beat for 1 more minute or 100 strokes.
5. Add ground almonds and almond extract and beat for 1 more minute or 100 strokes.
6. Pour into 2 greased, lightly floured 8-inch round cake tins.
7. Bake in a preheated 350° oven for 30 to 35 minutes.
8. Remove from pan and cool on a cake rack.
9. These single layer cakes should be served in the shape of a fruit. The cake can be frosted with apricot or currant jelly to resemble a peach or an apple. The apple signifies a long journey for peace. The peach means longevity. Cut indentations of the edge of each cake so that they look like peaches or apples. Add a flower stem and leaf.

CAKE OF GOOD FORTUNE II

Serves 4 to 6

6 egg yolks	½ cup bread crumbs
1 cup sugar	6 egg whites, beaten stiff
1 cup ground blanched almonds	½ tsp almond extract

METHOD

1. Add sugar to egg yolk. Beat until creamy.
2. Add almonds, bread crumbs, and extract. Mix thoroughly.
3. Fold in stiff egg whites. Pour into 8-inch round tins lined with wax paper.
4. Bake at 350° for 40 minutes. Cool in the pan. Cut into fruit shape. Garnish with flower stem and leaf.

CHAPTER 19

Some Ideas for Leftovers

FOOD is so sacred to the Chinese that they cannot bear to throw any of it away. They have learned to make tasty dishes out of leftovers. In fact some dishes such as fried rice (see our chapter on rice) require leftovers. They often plan their meals with leftovers in mind, thinking when they buy a ham or a chicken of the many roles it will play on the table. There is a saying that the Chinese can take the bark from the tree and the grass from the field and make them tasty and delicious. We won't go that far but we will give you some ideas on what to do with the usual leftovers in the refrigerator.

The first step in using leftovers is to package them in such a way that their flavor and quality are preserved. Preferably they should look fairly pleasant on the shelves of our refrigerator so that we will look forward to using them. The containers should be glass or ceramic since these materials are nonporous and easily cleaned and sterilized.

The Chinese sometimes use glass jars for leftovers. They have tight lids, they are neat, attractive, and they are free. Empty mayonnaise and peanut butter jars are fine for this purpose. Be sure that you do not leave foods outside the refrigerator in glass containers, however, since light destroys riboflavin.

In China, cooking ahead is a standard practice. Chinese menus contain a greater variety of dishes than is customary in the West, and it takes too much time to start everything from scratch. The Chinese usually plan their meals so that one night's dinner is the basis of a meal the next day. One night, for example, they will have fried fish and the next night sweet-sour fish.

SHERRY MEATBALLS WITH SPINACH (CELERY)

SERVES 4 to 6

METHOD: Hot frying

INGREDIENTS

1 to 2 lb leftover meatballs

1 cup uncooked spinach, cut in 2-inch lengths, or 2 cups celery, finely stripped

1 tsp cornstarch ⎤ Mix
2 Tbs water   ⎦ Thickening

CONDIMENTS

Mix Sauce ⎧ 2 Tbs soy sauce
          ⎪ 1 Tbs sherry
          ⎨ ½ tsp salt
          ⎪ ⅛ tsp MSG
          ⎩ ⅛ tsp pepper

1 Tbs peanut oil for frying
1 scallion or 1 dry onion
1 garlic clove, crushed
1 ginger, sliced

METHOD

1. Heat skillet (350°). Add oil, heat thoroughly.
2. Pour boiling water over spinach or celery before cooking.
3. Fry scallion, garlic, and ginger until light golden brown.
4. Add sauce and bring to boiling.
5. Add meatballs and simmer for 5 minutes.
6. Add spinach and cook for 2 minutes.
7. Add thickening and cook for 1 minute.

SWEET AND SOUR MEATBALLS

SERVES 4 to 6

METHOD: Hot frying

INGREDIENTS

1 to 2 lb leftover meatballs

2 Tbs cornstarch ⎤ Mix
2 Tbs water   ⎦ Thickening

CONDIMENTS

Mix Sauce ⎧ 2 Tbs soy sauce
          ⎪ 1 Tbs sherry
          ⎨ 2 Tbs vinegar
          ⎪ 4 Tbs sugar
          ⎪ ½ tsp salt
          ⎩ ⅛ tsp MSG

1 Tbs peanut oil for frying

METHOD

1. Heat skillet (350°). Add oil, heat thoroughly.
2. Fry garlic to light golden brown.
3. Add sauce and bring to boiling.
4. Add meatballs and simmer 5 minutes.
5. Add thickening and cook 1 minute.

MEATBALLS WITH CHINESE BARBECUE SAUCE

SERVES 4 to 6   METHOD: Hot frying

INGREDIENTS   **CONDIMENTS**

1 to 2 lb leftover meatballs

2 Tbs cornstarch	Mix
2 Tbs water	Thickening

Mix Sauce:
- 1 Tbs soy sauce
- 1 cup catsup
- 1 Tbs sherry
- 2 Tbs brown sugar
- ½ tsp salt
- ⅛ tsp MSG
- ⅛ tsp pepper

1 Tbs peanut oil for frying
1 garlic clove, crushed

METHOD

1. Heat skillet (350°). Add oil, heat thoroughly.
2. Fry garlic to light golden brown.
3. Add sauce and bring to boiling.
4. Add meatballs and simmer 5 minutes.
5. Add thickening and cook 1 minute.

ASPIC
(CHICKEN, PORK OR BEEF)

SERVES 4 to 6

INGREDIENTS

2 cups diced or shredded cooked
   chicken breast, pork, or beef
1 pkg clear gelatin
2 cups chicken, turkey, or beef stock

CONDIMENTS

Mix Sauce { 1 tsp soy sauce
1 tsp sherry
⅛ tsp MSG

METHOD

1. Soften gelatin in ¼ cup water.
2. Bring stock to a boil.
3. Add softened gelatin to hot stock. Mix well. Add sherry and soy
   sauce mixture.
4. Add cold meat to stock.
5. Pour in mold; jell in refrigerator.

CHINESE GOURMET SALAD

SERVES 4 to 6

INGREDIENTS

2 cups cold cooked chicken,
   stripped*
4 cups of stripped cucumber*
¼ dry onion stripped

CONDIMENTS

Mix Sauce { 1 Tbs soy sauce
1 Tbs sherry
½ tsp salt
⅛ tsp MSG
1 tsp sesame oil

METHOD

1. Mix ingredients well.
2. Add sauce. Stir thoroughly.
3. Put in refrigerator for 10 minutes.

* Any other meats, pork, beef, ham may be used. Celery or bean sprouts, can be
used in place of cucumber.

SWEET AND SOUR SEA FOOD

SERVES 4 to 6   METHOD: Hot frying

INGREDIENTS

4 cups leftover fish or shrimp*

2 Tbs cornstarch ⎱ Mix
2 Tbs water   ⎰ Thickening

CONDIMENTS

Mix
Sauce
⎰ 2 Tbs soy sauce
  1 Tbs sherry
  4 Tbs sugar
  1 tsp salt
  ⅛ tsp MSG
  4 Tbs vinegar
  1 clove garlic, crushed

METHOD

1. Heat skillet (300°). Add oil, heat thoroughly.
2. Fry garlic until light golden brown.
3. Add sauce and bring to boiling point.
4. Add fish or sea food and simmer 3 minutes.
5. Add thickening and cook 1 minute.

CONGEE

SERVES 4 to 6

INGREDIENTS

3 cups chicken stock   1 cup any leftover vegetables
3 cups water   2 to 4 cups cold cooked rice
2 cups chicken or other meat

METHOD

1. Heat chicken stock and water to boiling point.
2. Add meat and rice and bring to boiling point again.
3. Add vegetables and cook 3 minutes.

* Any leftover cooked fish or shrimp may be used. Leftover deep-fried fish are especially good.

POTATO PANCAKES

SERVES 4 to 6   METHOD: Hot frying

INGREDIENTS   ### CONDIMENTS

4 to 5 cups cooked potatoes,
   mashed

Mix Sauce:
- 3 Tbs soy sauce
- 1½ tsp salt
- ⅛ tsp MSG
- ⅛ tsp pepper

2 cups diced leftover cooked
   shrimp, crab, beef, pork, or
   chicken, diced

3 eggs, beaten

4 Tbs cornstarch

1 onion, minced

2 Tbs peanut oil for frying.
Add more if needed.

METHOD

1. Heat skillet (350°). Add oil, heat thoroughly.
2. Mix all ingredients and condiments together.
3. Form into pancakes 3 inches in diameter.
4. Brown on both sides.

Index

Acknowledgements

A BOOK of this kind is the work of many hands. I wish to express my appreciation to the many friends and students who have contributed to this book, aided in testing recipes and offered valuable criticisms. I especially wish to thank Professor and Mrs. John Ashby Conway, who have over the years offered encouragement in the writing of this book; Mrs. Macaulay Taylor, who has ably served as editor; and Miss Jessey Chida and Miss Margaret Welty, who have helped in the final reading and preparation of the manuscript.

My greatest debt is to my wife, May Lee, whose intimate knowledge of these culinary secrets is matched only by her patience and diligence in helping me write and prepare every phase of this book. The theoretical and practical virtues of this book are proffered by us jointly.

Seattle, Washington   LEE SU JAN
Summer, 1961